Table of Contents

Top 20 Test Taking Tips

1. Carefully follow all the test registration procedures
2. Know the test directions, duration, topics, question types, how many questions
3. Setup a flexible study schedule at least 3-4 weeks before test day
4. Study during the time of day you are most alert, relaxed, and stress free
5. Maximize your learning style; visual learner use visual study aids, auditory learner use auditory study aids
6. Focus on your weakest knowledge base
7. Find a study partner to review with and help clarify questions
8. Practice, practice, practice
9. Get a good night's sleep; don't try to cram the night before the test
10. Eat a well balanced meal
11. Know the exact physical location of the testing site; drive the route to the site prior to test day
12. Bring a set of ear plugs; the testing center could be noisy
13. Wear comfortable, loose fitting, layered clothing to the testing center; prepare for it to be either cold or hot during the test
14. Bring at least 2 current forms of ID to the testing center
15. Arrive to the test early; be prepared to wait and be patient
16. Eliminate the obviously wrong answer choices, then guess the first remaining choice
17. Pace yourself; don't rush, but keep working and move on if you get stuck
18. Maintain a positive attitude even if the test is going poorly
19. Keep your first answer unless you are positive it is wrong
20. Check your work, don't make a careless mistake

Mathematics Test

Pre-algebra and Algebra

Numbers and their Classifications

Numbers are the basic building blocks of mathematics. Specific features of numbers are identified by the following terms:

Integers – The set of whole positive and negative numbers, including zero. Integers do not include fractions ($\frac{1}{3}$), decimals (0.56), or mixed numbers ($7\frac{3}{4}$).

Prime number – A whole number greater than 1 that has only two factors, itself and 1; that is, a number that can be divided evenly only by 1 and itself.

Composite number – A whole number greater than 1 that has more than two different factors; in other words, any whole number that is not a prime number. For example: The composite number 8 has the factors of 1, 2, 4, and 8.

Even number – Any integer that can be divided by 2 without leaving a remainder. For example: 2, 4, 6, 8, and so on.

Odd number – Any integer that cannot be divided evenly by 2. For example: 3, 5, 7, 9, and so on.

Decimal number – a number that uses a decimal point to show the part of the number that is less than one. Example: 1.234.

Decimal point – a symbol used to separate the ones place from the tenths place in decimals or dollars from cents in currency.

Decimal place – the position of a number to the right of the decimal point. In the decimal 0.123, the 1 is in the first place to the right of the decimal point, indicating tenths; the 2 is in the second place, indicating hundredths; and the 3 is in the third place, indicating thousandths.

The decimal, or base 10, system is a number system that uses ten different digits (0, 1, 2, 3, 4, 5, 6, 7, 8, 9). An example of a number system that uses something other than ten digits is the binary, or base 2, number system, used by computers, which uses only the numbers 0 and 1. It is thought that the decimal system originated because people had only their 10 fingers for counting.

Rational, irrational, and real numbers can be described as follows:

Rational numbers include all integers, decimals, and fractions. Any terminating or repeating decimal number is a rational number.

Irrational numbers cannot be written as fractions or decimals because the number of decimal places is infinite and there is no recurring pattern of digits within the number. For example, pi (π) begins with 3.141592 and continues without terminating or repeating, so pi is an irrational number.

Real numbers are the set of all rational and irrational numbers.

Operations

There are four basic mathematical operations:

Addition increases the value of one quantity by the value of another quantity. Example: $2 + 4 = 6$; $8 + 9 = 17$. The result is called the sum. With addition, the order does not matter. $4 + 2 = 2 + 4$.

Subtraction is the opposite operation to addition; it decreases the value of one quantity by the value of another quantity. Example: $6 - 4 = 2$; $17 - 8 = 9$. The result is called the difference. Note that with subtraction, the order does matter. $6 - 4 \neq 4 - 6$.

Multiplication can be thought of as repeated addition. One number tells how many times to add the other number to itself. Example: 3×2 (three times two) $= 2 + 2 + 2 = 6$. With multiplication, the order does not matter. $2 \times 3 = 3 \times 2$ or $3 + 3 = 2 + 2 + 2$.

Division is the opposite operation to multiplication; one number tells us how many parts to divide the other number into. Example: $20 \div 4 = 5$; if 20 is split into 4 equal parts, each part is 5. With division, the order of the numbers does matter. $20 \div 4 \neq 4 \div 20$.

An exponent is a superscript number placed next to another number at the top right. It indicates how many times the base number is to be multiplied by itself. Exponents provide a shorthand way to write what would be a longer mathematical expression. Example: $a^2 = a \times a$; $2^4 = 2 \times 2 \times 2 \times 2$. A number with an exponent of 2 is said to be "squared," while a number with an exponent of 3 is said to be "cubed." The value of a number raised to an exponent is called its power. So, 8^4 is read as "8 to the 4th power," or "8 raised to the power of 4." A negative exponent is the same as the reciprocal of a positive exponent. Example: $a^{-2} = \frac{1}{a^2}$.

> ➤ **Review Video: Exponents**
> Visit ***mometrix.com/academy*** and enter ***Code: 600998***

Parentheses are used to designate which operations should be done first when there are multiple operations. Example: $4 - (2 + 1) = 1$; the parentheses tell us that we must add 2 and 1, and then subtract the sum from 4, rather than subtracting 2 from 4 and then adding 1 (this would give us an answer of 3).

Order of Operations is a set of rules that dictates the order in which we must perform each operation in an expression so that we will evaluate at accurately. If we have an expression that includes multiple different operations, Order of Operations tells us which operations to do first. The most common mnemonic for Order of Operations is PEMDAS, or "Please Excuse My Dear Aunt Sally." PEMDAS stands for Parentheses, Exponents, Multiplication, Division, Addition, Subtraction. It is important to understand that multiplication and division have equal precedence, as do addition and subtraction, so those pairs of operations are simply worked from left to right in order. Example: Evaluate the expression $5 + 20 \div 4 \times (2 + 3)^2 - 6$ using the correct order of operations. P: Perform the operations inside the parentheses, $(2 + 3) = 5$. E: Simplify the exponents, $(5)^2 = 25$. The equation now looks like this: $5 + 20 \div 4 \times 25 - 6$.

➤ **Review Video: Order of Operations**
Visit mometrix.com/academy and enter Code: 259675

MD: Perform multiplication and division from left to right, $20 \div 4 = 5$; then $5 \times 25 = 125$. The equation now looks like this: $5 + 125 - 6$.

AS: Perform addition and subtraction from left to right, $5 + 125 = 130$; then $130 - 6 = 124$.

The laws of exponents are as follows:

1) Any number to the power of 1 is equal to itself: $a^1 = a$.

2) The number 1 raised to any power is equal to 1: $1^n = 1$.

3) Any number raised to the power of 0 is equal to 1: $a^0 = 1$.

4) Add exponents to multiply powers of the same base number: $a^n \times a^m = a^{n+m}$.

5) Subtract exponents to divide powers of the same number; that is $a^n \div a^m = a^{n-m}$.

6) Multiply exponents to raise a power to a power: $(a^n)^m = a^{n \times m}$.

7) If multiplied or divided numbers inside parentheses are collectively raised to a power, this is the same as each individual term being raised to that power: $(a \times b)^n = a^n \times b^n$; $(a \div b)^n = a^n \div b^n$.

Note: Exponents do not have to be integers. Fractional or decimal exponents follow all the rules above as well. Example: $5^{\frac{1}{4}} \times 5^{\frac{3}{4}} = 5^{\frac{1}{4} + \frac{3}{4}} = 5^1 = 5$.

A root, such as a square root, is another way of writing a fractional exponent. Instead of using a superscript, roots use the radical symbol ($\sqrt{}$) to indicate the operation. A radical will have a number underneath the bar, and may sometimes have a number in the upper left: $\sqrt[n]{a}$, read as "the nth root of a." The relationship between radical notation and exponent notation can be described by this equation: $\sqrt[n]{a} = a^{\frac{1}{n}}$. The two special cases of $n = 2$ and $n = 3$ are called square roots and cube roots. If there is no number to the upper left, it is understood to be a square root ($n = 2$). Nearly all of the roots you encounter will be square roots. A square root is the same as a number raised to the one-half power. When we say that a is the square root of b ($a = \sqrt{b}$), we mean that a multiplied by itself equals b: ($a \times a = b$).

➤ **Review Video: Square Root and Perfect Square Explained**
Visit mometrix.com/academy and enter Code: 648063

A perfect square is a number that has an integer for its square root. There are 10 perfect squares from 1 to 100: 1, 4, 9, 16, 25, 36, 49, 64, 81, 100 (the squares of integers 1 through 10).

Scientific notation is a way of writing large numbers in a shorter form. The form $a \times 10^n$ is used in scientific notation, where a is greater than or equal to 1, but less than 10, and n is the number of places the decimal must move to get from the original number to a. Example: The number 230,400,000 is cumbersome to write. To write the value in scientific notation, place a decimal point between the first and second numbers, and include all digits through the last non-zero digit ($a = 2.304$). To find the appropriate power of 10, count the number of places the decimal point had to move ($n = 8$). The number is positive if the decimal moved to the left, and negative if it moved to the right. We can then write 230,400,000 as 2.304×10^8. If we look instead at the number 0.00002304, we have the same value for a, but this time the decimal moved 5 places to the right ($n = -5$). Thus, 0.00002304 can be written as 2.304×10^{-5}. Using this notation makes it simple to compare very large or very small numbers. By comparing exponents, it is easy to see that 3.28×10^4 is smaller than 1.51×10^5, because 4 is less than 5.

> ➤ **Review Video: <u>Scientific Notation Explained</u>**
> *Visit **mometrix.com/academy** and enter **Code: 976454***

Positive & Negative Numbers

A precursor to working with negative numbers is understanding what absolute values are. A number's *Absolute Value* is simply the distance away from zero a number is on the number line. The absolute value of a number is always positive and is written $|x|$.

When adding signed numbers, if the signs are the same simply add the absolute values of the addends and apply the original sign to the sum. For example, $(+4) + (+8) = +12$ and $(-4) + (-8) = -12$. When the original signs are different, take the absolute values of the addends and subtract the smaller value from the larger value, then apply the original sign of the larger value to the difference. For instance, $(+4) + (-8) = -4$ and $(-4) + (+8) = +4$.

For subtracting signed numbers, change the sign of the number after the minus symbol and then follow the same rules used for addition. For example, $(+4) - (+8) = (+4) + (-8) = -4$.

If the signs are the same the product is positive when multiplying signed numbers. For example, $(+4) \times (+8) = +32$ and $(-4) \times (-8) = +32$. If the signs are opposite, the product is negative. For example, $(+4) \times (-8) = -32$ and $(-4) \times (+8) = -32$. When more than two factors are multiplied together, the sign of the product is determined by how many negative factors are present. If there are an odd number of negative factors then the product is negative, whereas an even number of negative factors indicates a positive product. For instance, $(+4) \times (-8) \times (-2) = +64$ and $(-4) \times (-8) \times (-2) = -64$.

The rules for dividing signed numbers are similar to multiplying signed numbers. If the dividend and divisor have the same sign, the quotient is positive. If the dividend and divisor have opposite signs, the quotient is negative. For example, $(-4) \div (+8) = -0.5$.

Factors and Multiples

Factors are numbers that are multiplied together to obtain a product. For example, in the equation $2 \times 3 = 6$, the numbers 2 and 3 are factors. A prime number has only two factors (1 and itself), but other numbers can have many factors.
A common factor is a number that divides exactly into two or more other numbers. For example, the factors of 12 are 1, 2, 3, 4, 6, and 12, while the factors of 15 are 1, 3, 5, and 15. The common factors of 12 and 15 are 1 and 3.

A prime factor is also a prime number. Therefore, the prime factors of 12 are 2 and 3. For 15, the prime factors are 3 and 5.

The greatest common factor (GCF) is the largest number that is a factor of two or more numbers. For example, the factors of 15 are 1, 3, 5, and 15; the factors of 35 are 1, 5, 7, and 35. Therefore, the greatest common factor of 15 and 35 is 5.

The least common multiple (LCM) is the smallest number that is a multiple of two or more numbers. For example, the multiples of 3 include 3, 6, 9, 12, 15, etc.; the multiples of 5 include 5, 10, 15, 20, etc. Therefore, the least common multiple of 3 and 5 is 15.

> **Review Video: Greatest Common Factor (GCF)**
> *Visit **mometrix.com/academy** and enter **Code: 838699***

Fractions, Percentages, and Related Concepts

A fraction is a number that is expressed as one integer written above another integer, with a dividing line between them ($\frac{x}{y}$). It represents the quotient of the two numbers "x divided by y." It can also be thought of as x out of y equal parts.

The top number of a fraction is called the numerator, and it represents the number of parts under consideration. The 1 in $\frac{1}{4}$ means that 1 part out of the whole is being considered in the calculation. The bottom number of a fraction is called the denominator, and it represents the total number of equal parts. The 4 in $\frac{1}{4}$ means that the whole consists of 4 equal parts. A fraction cannot have a denominator of zero; this is referred to as "undefined."

> **Review Video: Fractions**
> *Visit **mometrix.com/academy** and enter **Code: 262335***

Fractions can be manipulated, without changing the value of the fraction, by multiplying or dividing (but not adding or subtracting) both the numerator and denominator by the same number. If you divide both numbers by a common factor, you are reducing or simplifying the fraction. Two fractions that have the same value, but are expressed differently are known as equivalent fractions. For example, $\frac{2}{10}, \frac{3}{15}, \frac{4}{20}$, and $\frac{5}{25}$ are all equivalent fractions. They can also all be reduced or simplified to $\frac{1}{5}$.

When two fractions are manipulated so that they have the same denominator, this is known as finding a common denominator. The number chosen to be that common denominator should be the least common multiple of the two original denominators. Example: $\frac{3}{4}$ and $\frac{5}{6}$; the least common multiple of 4 and 6 is 12. Manipulating to achieve the common denominator: $\frac{3}{4} = \frac{9}{12}; \frac{5}{6} = \frac{10}{12}$.

If two fractions have a common denominator, they can be added or subtracted simply by adding or subtracting the two numerators and retaining the same denominator. Example: $\frac{1}{2} + \frac{1}{4} = \frac{2}{4} + \frac{1}{4} = \frac{3}{4}$. If the two fractions do not already have the same denominator, one or both of them must be manipulated to achieve a common denominator before they can be added or subtracted.

Two fractions can be multiplied by multiplying the two numerators to find the new numerator and the two denominators to find the new denominator. Example: $\frac{1}{3} \times \frac{2}{3} = \frac{1\times2}{3\times3} = \frac{2}{9}$.

> ➢ **Review Video: Multiplying Fractions**
> *Visit **mometrix.com/academy** and enter **Code: 638849***

Two fractions can be divided flipping the numerator and denominator of the second fraction and then proceeding as though it were a multiplication. Example: $\frac{2}{3} \div \frac{3}{4} = \frac{2}{3} \times \frac{4}{3} = \frac{8}{9}$.

> ➢ **Review Video: Dividing Fractions**
> *Visit **mometrix.com/academy** and enter **Code: 300874***

A fraction whose denominator is greater than its numerator is known as a proper fraction, while a fraction whose numerator is greater than its denominator is known as an improper fraction. Proper fractions have values less than one and improper fractions have values greater than one.

A mixed number is a number that contains both an integer and a fraction. Any improper fraction can be rewritten as a mixed number. Example: $\frac{8}{3} = \frac{6}{3} + \frac{2}{3} = 2 + \frac{2}{3} = 2\frac{2}{3}$. Similarly, any mixed number can be rewritten as an improper fraction. Example: $1\frac{3}{5} = 1 + \frac{3}{5} = \frac{5}{5} + \frac{3}{5} = \frac{8}{5}$.

> ➢ **Review Video: Improper Fractions and Mixed Numbers**
> *Visit **mometrix.com/academy** and enter **Code: 731507***

Percentages can be thought of as fractions that are based on a whole of 100; that is, one whole is equal to 100%. The word percent means "per hundred." Fractions can be expressed as percents by finding equivalent fractions with a denominator of 100. Example: $\frac{7}{10} = \frac{70}{100} = 70\%$; $\frac{1}{4} = \frac{25}{100} = 25\%$. To express a percentage as a fraction, divide the percentage number by 100 and reduce the fraction to its simplest possible terms. Example: $60\% = \frac{60}{100} = \frac{3}{5}$; $96\% = \frac{96}{100} = \frac{24}{25}$.

Converting decimals to percentages and percentages to decimals is as simple as moving the decimal point. To convert from a decimal to a percent, move the decimal point two places to the right. To convert from a percent to a decimal, move it two places to the left. Example: 0.23 = 23%; 5.34 = 534%; 0.007 = 0.7%; 700% = 7.00; 86% = 0.86; 0.15% = 0.0015.

It may be helpful to remember that the percentage number will always be larger than the equivalent decimal number.

A percentage problem can be presented three main ways: (1) Find what percentage of some number another number is. Example: What percentage of 40 is 8? (2) Find what number is some percentage of a given number. Example: What number is 20% of 40? (3) Find what number another number is a given percentage of. Example: What number is 8 20% of? The three components in all of these cases are the same: a whole (W), a part (P), and a percentage (%). These are related by the equation: $P = W \times \%$. This is the form of the equation you would use to solve problems of type (2). To solve types (1) and (3), you would use these two forms: $\% = \frac{P}{W}$ and $W = \frac{P}{\%}$.

> ➢ **Review Video: <u>Percentages Explained</u>**
> *Visit **mometrix.com/academy** and enter **Code: 141911***

The thing that frequently makes percentage problems difficult is that they are most often also word problems, so a large part of solving them is figuring out which quantities are what. Example: In a school cafeteria, 7 students choose pizza, 9 choose hamburgers, and 4 choose tacos. Find the percentage that chooses tacos. To find the whole, you must first add all of the parts: 7 + 9 + 4 = 20. The percentage can then be found by dividing the part by the whole ($\% = \frac{P}{W}$): $\frac{4}{20} = \frac{20}{100} = 20\%$.

A ratio is a comparison of two quantities in a particular order. Example: If there are 14 computers in a lab, and the class has 20 students, there is a student to computer ratio of 20 to 14, commonly written as 20:14. Ratios are normally reduced to their smallest whole number representation, so 20:14 would be reduced to 10:7 by dividing both sides by 2.

A proportion is a relationship between two quantities that dictates how one changes when the other changes. A direct proportion describes a relationship in which a quantity increases by a set amount for every increase in the other quantity, or decreases by that same amount for every decrease in the other quantity. Example: Assuming a constant driving speed, the time required for a car trip increases as the distance of the trip increases. The distance to be traveled and the time required to travel are directly proportional.

Inverse proportion is a relationship in which an increase in one quantity is accompanied by a decrease in the other, or vice versa. Example: the time required for a car trip decreases as the speed increases, and increases as the speed decreases, so the time required is inversely proportional to the speed of the car.

Equations and Graphing

When algebraic functions and equations are shown graphically, they are usually shown on a *Cartesian Coordinate Plane*. The Cartesian coordinate plane consists of two number lines placed perpendicular to each other, and intersecting at the zero point, also known as the origin. The horizontal number line is known as the *x*-axis, with positive values to the right of the origin, and negative values to the left of the origin. The vertical number line is known as the *y*-axis, with positive values above the origin, and negative values below the origin. Any point on the plane can be identified by an ordered pair in the form (x,y), called coordinates. The x-value of the coordinate is called the abscissa, and the y-value of the coordinate is called the ordinate. The two number lines divide the plane into four quadrants: I, II, III, and IV.

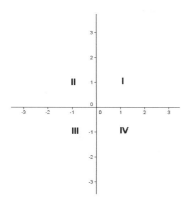

Before learning the different forms equations can be written in, it is important to understand some terminology. A ratio of the change in the vertical distance to the change in horizontal distance is called the *Slope*. On a graph with two points, (x_1, y_1) and (x_2, y_2), the slope is represented by the formula $= \frac{y_2 - y_1}{x_2 - x_1}$; $x_1 \neq x_2$. If the value of the slope is positive, the line slopes upward from left to right. If the value of the slope is negative, the line slopes downward from left to right. If the y-coordinates are the same for both points, the slope is 0 and the line is a *Horizontal Line*. If the x-coordinates are the same for both points, there is no slope and the line is a *Vertical Line*. Two or more lines that have equal slopes are *Parallel Lines*. *Perpendicular Lines* have slopes that are negative reciprocals of each other, such as $\frac{a}{b}$ and $\frac{-b}{a}$.

Equations are made up of monomials and polynomials. A *Monomial* is a single variable or product of constants and variables, such as x, $2x$, or $\frac{2}{x}$. There will never be addition or subtraction symbols in a monomial. Like monomials have like variables, but they may have different coefficients. *Polynomials* are algebraic expressions which use addition and subtraction to combine two or more monomials. Two terms make a binomial; three terms make a trinomial; etc.. The *Degree of a Monomial* is the sum of the exponents of the variables. The *Degree of a Polynomial* is the highest degree of any individual term.

As mentioned previously, equations can be written many ways. Below is a list of the many forms equations can take.

- *Standard Form*: $Ax + By = C$; the slope is $\frac{-A}{B}$ and the y-intercept is $\frac{C}{B}$
- *Slope Intercept Form*: $y = mx + b$, where m is the slope and b is the y-intercept
- *Point-Slope Form*: $y - y_1 = m(x - x_1)$, where m is the slope and (x_1, y_1) is a point on the line
- *Two-Point Form*: $\frac{y - y_1}{x - x_1} = \frac{y_2 - y_1}{x_2 - x_1}$, where (x_1, y_1) and (x_2, y_2) are two points on the given line

- *Intercept Form*: $\frac{x}{x_1} + \frac{y}{y_1} = 1$, where $(x_1, 0)$ is the point at which a line intersects the x-axis, and $(0, y_1)$ is the point at which the same line intersects the y-axis

➢ **Review Video: Slope Intercept and Point-Slope Forms**
*Visit **mometrix.com/academy** and enter **Code: 113216***

Equations can also be written as $ax + b = 0$, where $a \neq 0$. These are referred to as *One Variable Linear Equations*. A solution to such an equation is called a *Root*. In the case where we have the equation $5x + 10 = 0$, if we solve for x we get a solution of $x = -2$. In other words, the root of the equation is -2. This is found by first subtracting 10 from both sides, which gives $5x = -10$. Next, simply divide both sides by the coefficient of the variable, in this case 5, to get $x = -2$. This can be checked by plugging -2 back into the original equation $(5)(-2) + 10 = -10 + 10 = 0$.

The *Solution Set* is the set of all solutions of an equation. In our example, the solution set would simply be -2. If there were more solutions (there usually are in multivariable equations) then they would also be included in the solution set. When an equation has no true solutions, this is referred to as an *Empty Set*. Equations with identical solution sets are *Equivalent Equations*. An *Identity* is a term whose value or determinant is equal to 1.

Other Important Concepts

Commonly in algebra and other upper-level fields of math you find yourself working with mathematical expressions that do not equal each other. The statement comparing such expressions with symbols such as < (less than) or > (greater than) is called an *Inequality*. An example of an inequality is $7x > 5$. To solve for x, simply divide both sides by 7 and the solution is shown to be $x > \frac{5}{7}$. Graphs of the solution set of inequalities are represented on a number line. Open circles are used to show that an expression approaches a number but is never quite equal to that number.

➢ **Review Video: Inequalities**
*Visit **mometrix.com/academy** and enter **Code: 451494***

Conditional Inequalities are those with certain values for the variable that will make the condition true and other values for the variable where the condition will be false. *Absolute Inequalities* can have any real number as the value for the variable to make the condition true, while there is no real number value for the variable that will make the condition false. Solving inequalities is done by following the same rules as for solving equations with the exception that when multiplying or dividing by a negative number the direction of the inequality sign must be flipped or reversed. *Double Inequalities* are situations where two inequality statements apply to the same variable expression. An example of this is $-c < ax + b < c$.

A *Weighted Mean*, or weighted average, is a mean that uses "weighted" values. The formula is weighted mean $= \frac{w_1 x_1 + w_2 x_2 + w_3 x_3 \ldots + w_n x_n}{w_1 + w_2 + w_3 + \cdots + w_n}$. Weighted values, such as $w_1, w_2, w_3, \ldots w_n$ are assigned to each member of the set $x_1, x_2, x_3, \ldots x_n$. If calculating weighted mean, make sure a weight value for each member of the set is used.

Calculations Using Points

Sometimes you need to perform calculations using only points on a graph as input data. Using points, you can determine what the midpoint and distance are. If you know the equation for a line you can calculate the distance between the line and the point.

To find the *Midpoint* of two points (x_1, y_1) and (x_2, y_2), average the x-coordinates to get the x-coordinate of the midpoint, and average the y-coordinates to get the y-coordinate of the midpoint. The formula is midpoint $= \left(\frac{x_1+x_2}{2}, \frac{y_1+y_2}{2}\right)$.

The *Distance* between two points is the same as the length of the hypotenuse of a right triangle with the two given points as endpoints, and the two sides of the right triangle parallel to the x-axis and y-axis, respectively. The length of the segment parallel to the x-axis is the difference between the x-coordinates of the two points. The length of the segment parallel to the y-axis is the difference between the y-coordinates of the two points. Use the Pythagorean Theorem $a^2 + b^2 = c^2$ or $c = \sqrt{a^2 + b^2}$ to find the distance. The formula is: distance $= \sqrt{(x_2 - x_1)^2 + (y_2 - y_1)^2}$.

When a line is in the format $Ax + By + C = 0$, where A, B, and C are coefficients, you can use a point (x_1, y_1) not on the line and apply the formula $d = \frac{|Ax_1 + By_1 + C|}{\sqrt{A^2 + B^2}}$ to find the distance between the line and the point (x_1, y_1).

Systems of Equations

Systems of Equations are a set of simultaneous equations that all use the same variables. A solution to a system of equations must be true for each equation in the system. *Consistent Systems* are those with at least one solution. *Inconsistent Systems* are systems of equations that have no solution.

> ➢ **Review Video: Systems of Equations**
> Visit **mometrix.com/academy** and enter **Code: 658153**

To solve a system of linear equations by *substitution*, start with the easier equation and solve for one of the variables. Express this variable in terms of the other variable. Substitute this expression in the other equation, and solve for the other variable. The solution should be expressed in the form (x, y). Substitute the values into both of the original equations to check your answer. Consider the following problem.

Solve the system using substitution:
$x + 6y = 15$
$3x - 12y = 18$

Solve the first equation for x:
$$x = 15 - 6y$$

Substitute this value in place of x in the second equation, and solve for y:
$$3(15 - 6y) - 12y = 18$$
$$45 - 18y - 12y = 18$$
$$30y = 27$$
$$y = \frac{27}{30} = \frac{9}{10} = 0.9$$

Plug this value for y back into the first equation to solve for x:
$$x = 15 - 6(0.9) = 15 - 5.4 = 9.6$$

Check both equations if you have time:
$$9.6 + 6(0.9) = 9.6 + 5.4 = 15$$
$$3(9.6) - 12(0.9) = 28.8 - 10.8 = 18$$
Therefore, the solution is $(9.6, 0.9)$.

To solve a system of equations using *elimination*, begin by rewriting both equations in standard form $Ax + By = C$. Check to see if the coefficients of one pair of like variables add to zero. If not, multiply one or both of the equations by a non-zero number to make one set of like variables add to zero. Add the two equations to solve for one of the variables. Substitute this value into one of the original equations to solve for the other variable. Check your work by substituting into the other equation. Next we will solve the same problem as above, but using the addition method.

Solve the system using elimination:
$$x + 6y = 15$$
$$3x - 12y = 18$$

If we multiply the first equation by 2, we can eliminate the y terms:
$$2x + 12y = 30$$
$$3x - 12y = 18$$

Add the equations together and solve for x:
$$5x = 48$$
$$x = \frac{48}{5} = 9.6$$

Plug the value for x back into either of the original equations and solve for y:
$$9.6 + 6y = 15$$
$$y = \frac{15 - 9.6}{6} = 0.9$$

Check both equations if you have time:
$$9.6 + 6(0.9) = 9.6 + 5.4 = 15$$
$$3(9.6) - 12(0.9) = 28.8 - 10.8 = 18$$
Therefore, the solution is $(9.6, 0.9)$.

Polynomial Algebra

To multiply two binomials, follow the *FOIL* method. FOIL stands for:

- First: Multiply the first term of each binomial
- Outer: Multiply the outer terms of each binomial
- Inner: Multiply the inner terms of each binomial
- Last: Multiply the last term of each binomial

Using FOIL, $(Ax + By)(Cx + Dy) = ACx^2 + ADxy + BCxy + BDy^2$.

> ➤ **Review Video: Multiplying Terms Using the FOIL Method**
> Visit **mometrix.com/academy** and enter **Code: 854792**

To divide polynomials, begin by arranging the terms of each polynomial in order of one variable. You may arrange in ascending or descending order, but be consistent with both polynomials. To get the first term of the quotient, divide the first term of the dividend by the first term of the divisor. Multiply the first term of the quotient by the entire divisor and subtract that product from the dividend. Repeat for the second and successive terms until you either get a remainder of zero or a remainder whose degree is less than the degree of the divisor. If the quotient has a remainder, write the answer as a mixed expression in the form: quotient $+ \frac{\text{remainder}}{\text{divisor}}$.

Rational Expressions are fractions with polynomials in both the numerator and the denominator; the value of the polynomial in the denominator cannot be equal to zero. To add or subtract rational expressions, first find the common denominator, then rewrite each fraction as an equivalent fraction with the common denominator. Finally, add or subtract the numerators to get the numerator of the answer, and keep the common denominator as the denominator of the answer. When multiplying rational expressions factor each polynomial and cancel like factors (a factor which appears in both the numerator and the denominator). Then, multiply all remaining factors in the numerator to get the numerator of the product, and multiply the remaining factors in the denominator to get the denominator of the product. Remember – cancel entire factors, not individual terms. To divide rational expressions, take the reciprocal of the divisor (the rational expression you are dividing by) and multiply by the dividend.

Below are patterns of some special products to remember: *perfect trinomial squares*, the *difference between two squares*, the *sum and difference of two cubes*, and *perfect cubes*.

- Perfect Trinomial Squares: $x^2 + 2xy + y^2 = (x + y)^2$ or $x^2 - 2xy + y^2 = (x - y)^2$

- 16 -

- Difference Between Two Squares: $x^2 - y^2 = (x + y)(x - y)$
- Sum of Two Cubes: $x^3 + y^3 = (x + y)(x^2 - xy + y^2)$
  Note: the second factor is NOT the same as a perfect trinomial square, so do not try to factor it further.
- Difference Between Two Cubes: $x^3 - y^3 = (x - y)(x^2 + xy + y^2)$
  Again, the second factor is NOT the same as a perfect trinomial square.
- Perfect Cubes: $x^3 + 3x^2y + 3xy^2 + y^3 = (x + y)^3$ and $x^3 - 3x^2y + 3xy^2 - y^3 = (x - y)^3$

In order to *factor* a polynomial, first check for a common monomial factor. When the greatest common monomial factor has been factored out, look for patterns of special products: differences of two squares, the sum or difference of two cubes for binomial factors, or perfect trinomial squares for trinomial factors. If the factor is a trinomial but not a perfect trinomial square, look for a factorable form, such as $x^2 + (a + b)x + ab = (x + a)(x + b)$ or $(ac)x^2 + (ad + bc)x + bd = (ax + b)(cx + d)$. For factors with four terms, look for groups to factor. Once you have found the factors, write the original polynomial as the product of all the factors. Make sure all of the polynomial factors are prime. Monomial factors may be prime or composite. Check your work by multiplying the factors to make sure you get the original polynomial.

Solving Quadratic Equations
The *Quadratic Formula* is used to solve quadratic equations when other methods are more difficult. To use the quadratic formula to solve a quadratic equation, begin by rewriting the equation in standard form $ax^2 + bx + c = 0$, where a, b, and c are coefficients. Once you have identified the values of the coefficients, substitute those values into the quadratic formula $= \frac{-b \pm \sqrt{b^2 - 4ac}}{2a}$. Evaluate the equation and simplify the expression. Again, check each root by substituting into the original equation. In the quadratic formula, the portion of the formula under the radical ($b^2 - 4ac$) is called the *Discriminant*. If the discriminant is zero, there is only one root: zero. If the discriminant is positive, there are two different real roots. If the discriminant is negative, there are no real roots.

To solve a quadratic equation by *Factoring*, begin by rewriting the equation in standard form, if necessary. Factor the side with the variable then set each of the factors equal to zero and solve the resulting linear equations. Check your answers by substituting the roots you found into the original equation. If, when writing the equation in standard form, you have an equation in the form $x^2 + c = 0$ or $x^2 - c = 0$, set $x^2 = -c$ or $x^2 = c$ and take the square root of c. If $c = 0$, the only real root is zero. If c is positive, there are two real roots—the positive and negative square root values. If c is negative, there are no real roots because you cannot take the square root of a negative number.

➢ **Review Video: Factoring Quadratic Equations**
*Visit **mometrix.com/academy** and enter **Code: 336566***

To solve a quadratic equation by *Completing the Square*, rewrite the equation so that all terms containing the variable are on the left side of the equal sign, and all the constants are on the right side of the equal sign. Make sure the coefficient of the squared term is 1. If there is a coefficient with the squared term, divide each term on both sides of the equal side by that number. Next, work with the coefficient of the single-variable term. Square half of this coefficient, and add that value to both sides. Now you can factor the left side (the side containing the variable) as the square of a binomial. $x^2 + 2ax + a^2 = C \Rightarrow (x + a)^2 = C$, where x is the variable, and a and C are constants. Take the square root of both sides and solve for the variable. Substitute the value of the variable in the original problem to check your work.

Geometry

Lines and Planes

A point is a fixed location in space; has no size or dimensions; commonly represented by a dot.

A line is a set of points that extends infinitely in two opposite directions. It has length, but no width or depth. A line can be defined by any two distinct points that it contains. A line segment is a portion of a line that has definite endpoints. A ray is a portion of a line that extends from a single point on that line in one direction along the line. It has a definite beginning, but no ending.

A plane is a two-dimensional flat surface defined by three non-collinear points. A plane extends an infinite distance in all directions in those two dimensions. It contains an infinite number of points, parallel lines and segments, intersecting lines and segments, as well as parallel or intersecting rays. A plane will never contain a three-dimensional figure or skew lines. Two given planes will either be parallel or they will intersect to form a line. A plane may intersect a circular conic surface, such as a cone, to form conic sections, such as the parabola, hyperbola, circle or ellipse.

Perpendicular lines are lines that intersect at right angles. They are represented by the symbol ⊥. The shortest distance from a line to a point not on the line is a perpendicular segment from the point to the line.

Parallel lines are lines in the same plane that have no points in common and never meet. It is possible for lines to be in different planes, have no points in common, and never meet, but they are not parallel because they are in different planes.

A bisector is a line or line segment that divides another line segment into two equal lengths. A perpendicular bisector of a line segment is composed of points that are equidistant from the endpoints of the segment it is dividing.

Intersecting lines are lines that have exactly one point in common. Concurrent lines are multiple lines that intersect at a single point.

A transversal is a line that intersects at least two other lines, which may or may not be parallel to one another. A transversal that intersects parallel lines is a common occurrence in geometry.

Angles

An angle is formed when two lines or line segments meet at a common point. It may be a common starting point for a pair of segments or rays, or it may be the intersection of lines. Angles are represented by the symbol ∠.

The vertex is the point at which two segments or rays meet to form an angle. If the angle is formed by intersecting rays, lines, and/or line segments, the vertex is the point at which four angles are formed. The pairs of angles opposite one another are called vertical angles, and their measures are equal.

An acute angle is an angle with a degree measure less than 90°.
A right angle is an angle with a degree measure of exactly 90°.
An obtuse angle is an angle with a degree measure greater than 90° but less than 180°.
A straight angle is an angle with a degree measure of exactly 180°. This is also a semicircle.
A reflex angle is an angle with a degree measure greater than 180° but less than 360°.
A full angle is an angle with a degree measure of exactly 360°.

> ➤ **Review Video: Geometric Symbols: Angles**
> *Visit **mometrix.com/academy** and enter **Code: 452738***

Two angles whose sum is exactly 90° are said to be complementary. The two angles may or may not be adjacent. In a right triangle, the two acute angles are complementary.

Two angles whose sum is exactly 180° are said to be supplementary. The two angles may or may not be adjacent. Two intersecting lines always form two pairs of supplementary angles. Adjacent supplementary angles will always form a straight line.

Two angles that have the same vertex and share a side are said to be adjacent. Vertical angles are not adjacent because they share a vertex but no common side.

Adjacent
Share vertex and side

Not adjacent
Share part of side, but not vertex

When two parallel lines are cut by a transversal, the angles that are between the two parallel lines are interior angles. In the diagram below, angles 3, 4, 5, and 6 are interior angles.

When two parallel lines are cut by a transversal, the angles that are outside the parallel lines are exterior angles. In the diagram below, angles 1, 2, 7, and 8 are exterior angles.

When two parallel lines are cut by a transversal, the angles that are in the same position relative to the transversal and a parallel line are corresponding angles. The diagram below has four pairs of corresponding angles: angles 1 and 5; angles 2 and 6; angles 3 and 7; and angles 4 and 8. Corresponding angles formed by parallel lines are congruent.

When two parallel lines are cut by a transversal, the two interior angles that are on opposite sides of the transversal are called alternate interior angles. In the diagram below, there are two pairs of alternate interior angles: angles 3 and 6, and angles 4 and 5. Alternate interior angles formed by parallel lines are congruent.

When two parallel lines are cut by a transversal, the two exterior angles that are on opposite sides of the transversal are called alternate exterior angles. In the diagram below, there are two pairs of alternate exterior angles: angles 1 and 8, and angles 2 and 7. Alternate exterior angles formed by parallel lines are congruent.

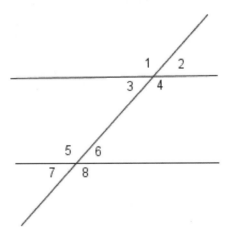

When two lines intersect, four angles are formed. The non-adjacent angles at this vertex are called vertical angles. Vertical angles are congruent. In the diagram, $\angle ABD \cong \angle CBE$ and $\angle ABC \cong \angle DBE$.

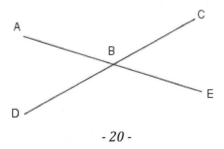

Triangles

An equilateral triangle is a triangle with three congruent sides. An equilateral triangle will also have three congruent angles, each 60°. All equilateral triangles are also acute triangles.

An isosceles triangle is a triangle with two congruent sides. An isosceles triangle will also have two congruent angles opposite the two congruent sides.

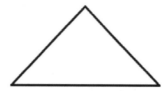

A scalene triangle is a triangle with no congruent sides. A scalene triangle will also have three angles of different measures. The angle with the largest measure is opposite the longest side, and the angle with the smallest measure is opposite the shortest side.

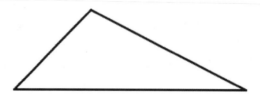

An acute triangle is a triangle whose three angles are all less than 90°. If two of the angles are equal, the acute triangle is also an isosceles triangle. If the three angles are all equal, the acute triangle is also an equilateral triangle.

A right triangle is a triangle with exactly one angle equal to 90°. All right triangles follow the Pythagorean Theorem. A right triangle can never be acute or obtuse.

An obtuse triangle is a triangle with exactly one angle greater than 90°. The other two angles may or may not be equal. If the two remaining angles are equal, the obtuse triangle is also an isosceles triangle.

Terminology

Altitude of a Triangle: A line segment drawn from one vertex perpendicular to the opposite side. In the diagram below, $\overline{BE}$, $\overline{AD}$, and $\overline{CF}$ are altitudes. The three altitudes in a triangle are always concurrent.

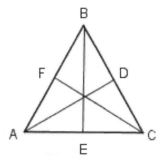

Height of a Triangle: The length of the altitude, although the two terms are often used interchangeably.

Orthocenter of a Triangle: The point of concurrency of the altitudes of a triangle. Note that in an obtuse triangle, the orthocenter will be outside the circle, and in a right triangle, the orthocenter is the vertex of the right angle.

Median of a Triangle: A line segment drawn from one vertex to the midpoint of the opposite side. This is not the same as the altitude, except the altitude to the base of an isosceles triangle and all three altitudes of an equilateral triangle.

Centroid of a Triangle: The point of concurrency of the medians of a triangle. This is the same point as the orthocenter only in an equilateral triangle. Unlike the orthocenter, the centroid is always inside the triangle. The centroid can also be considered the exact center of the triangle. Any shape triangle can be perfectly balanced on a tip placed at the centroid. The centroid is also the point that is two-thirds the distance from the vertex to the opposite side.

Pythagorean Theorem
The side of a triangle opposite the right angle is called the hypotenuse. The other two sides are called the legs. The Pythagorean Theorem states a relationship among the legs and hypotenuse of a right triangle: $a^2 + b^2 = c^2$, where a and b are the lengths of the legs of a right triangle, and c is the length of the hypotenuse. Note that this formula will only work with right triangles.

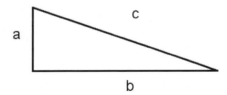

General rules

The Triangle Inequality Theorem states that the sum of the measures of any two sides of a triangle is always greater than the measure of the third side. If the sum of the measures of two sides were equal to the third side, a triangle would be impossible because the two sides would lie flat across the third side and there would be no vertex. If the sum of the measures of two of the sides was less than the third side, a closed figure would be impossible because the two shortest sides would never meet.

The sum of the measures of the interior angles of a triangle is always 180°. Therefore, a triangle can never have more than one angle greater than or equal to 90°.

In any triangle, the angles opposite congruent sides are congruent, and the sides opposite congruent angles are congruent. The largest angle is always opposite the longest side, and the smallest angle is always opposite the shortest side.

The line segment that joins the midpoints of any two sides of a triangle is always parallel to the third side and exactly half the length of the third side.

Similarity and congruence rules
Similar triangles are triangles whose corresponding angles are equal and whose corresponding sides are proportional. Represented by AA. Similar triangles whose corresponding sides are congruent are also congruent triangles.

> ➢ **Review Video: Similar Triangles**
> *Visit **mometrix.com/academy** and enter **Code: 398538***

Three sides of one triangle are congruent to the three corresponding sides of the second triangle. Represented as SSS.

Two sides and the included angle (the angle formed by those two sides) of one triangle are congruent to the corresponding two sides and included angle of the second triangle. Represented by SAS.

Two angles and the included side (the side that joins the two angles) of one triangle are congruent to the corresponding two angles and included side of the second triangle. Represented by ASA.

Two angles and a non-included side of one triangle are congruent to the corresponding two angles and non-included side of the second triangle. Represented by AAS.

Note that AAA is not a form for congruent triangles. This would say that the three angles are congruent, but says nothing about the sides. This meets the requirements for similar triangles, but not congruent triangles.

Area and perimeter formulas

The perimeter of any triangle is found by summing the three side lengths; $P = a + b + c$. For an equilateral triangle, this is the same as $P = 3s$, where s is any side length, since all three sides are the same length.

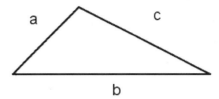

The area of any triangle can be found by taking half the product of one side length (base or b) and the perpendicular distance from that side to the opposite vertex (height or h). In equation form, $A = \frac{1}{2}bh$. For many triangles, it may be difficult to calculate h, so using one of the other formulas given here may be easier.

Another formula that works for any triangle is $A = \sqrt{s(s-a)(s-b)(s-c)}$, where A is the area, s is the semiperimeter $s = \frac{a+b+c}{2}$, and a, b, and c are the lengths of the three sides.

The area of an equilateral triangle can found by the formula $A = \frac{\sqrt{3}}{4}s^2$, where A is the area and s is the length of a side. You could use the $30° - 60° - 90°$ ratios to find the height of the triangle and then use the standard triangle area formula, but this is faster.

The area of an isosceles triangle can found by the formula, $A = \frac{1}{2}b\sqrt{a^2 - \frac{b^2}{4}}$, where A is the area, b is the base (the unique side), and a is the length of one of the two congruent sides. If you do not remember this formula, you can use the Pythagorean Theorem to find the height so you can use the standard formula for the area of a triangle.

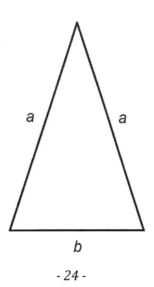

Trigonometric formulas

In the diagram below, angle C is the right angle, and side c is the hypotenuse. Side a is the side adjacent to angle B and side b is the side adjacent to angle A. These formulas will work for any acute angle in a right triangle. They will NOT work for any triangle that is not a right triangle. Also, they will not work for the right angle in a right triangle, since there are not distinct adjacent and opposite sides to differentiate from the hypotenuse.

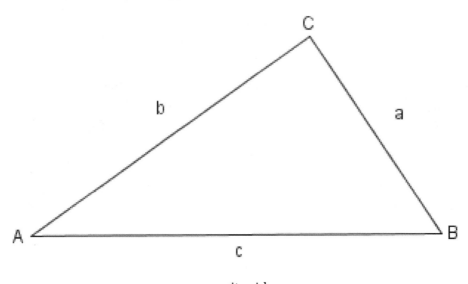

$$\sin A = \frac{\text{opposite side}}{\text{hypotenuse}} = \frac{a}{c}$$

$$\cos A = \frac{\text{adjacent side}}{\text{hypotenuse}} = \frac{b}{c}$$

$$\tan A = \frac{\text{opposite side}}{\text{adjacent side}} = \frac{a}{b}$$

$$\csc A = \frac{1}{\sin A} = \frac{\text{hypotenuse}}{\text{opposite side}} = \frac{c}{a}$$

$$\sec A = \frac{1}{\cos A} = \frac{\text{hypotenuse}}{\text{adjacent side}} = \frac{c}{b}$$

$$\cot A = \frac{1}{\tan A} = \frac{\text{adjacent side}}{\text{opposite side}} = \frac{b}{a}$$

Laws of Sines and Cosines

The Law of Sines states that $\frac{\sin A}{a} = \frac{\sin B}{b} = \frac{\sin C}{c}$, where A, B, and C are the angles of a triangle, and a, b, and c are the sides opposite their respective angles. This formula will work with all triangles, not just right triangles.

The Law of Cosines is given by the formula $c^2 = a^2 + b^2 - 2ab(\cos C)$, where a, b, and c are the sides of a triangle, and C is the angle opposite side c. This formula is similar to the Pythagorean Theorem, but unlike the Pythagorean Theorem, it can be used on any triangle.

Polygons

Each straight line segment of a polygon is called a side.

The point at which two sides of a polygon intersect is called the vertex. In a polygon, the number of sides is always equal to the number of vertices.

A polygon with all sides congruent and all angles equal is called a regular polygon.
A line segment from the center of a polygon perpendicular to a side of the polygon is called the apothem. In a regular polygon, the apothem can be used to find the area of the polygon using the formula $A = \frac{1}{2}ap$, where a is the apothem and p is the perimeter.

A line segment from the center of a polygon to a vertex of the polygon is called a radius. The radius of a regular polygon is also the radius of a circle that can be circumscribed about the polygon.

Triangle – 3 sides
Quadrilateral – 4 sides
Pentagon – 5 sides
Hexagon – 6 sides
Heptagon – 7 sides
Octagon – 8 sides
Nonagon – 9 sides
Decagon – 10 sides
Dodecagon – 12 sides

More generally, an n-gon is a polygon that has n angles and n sides.

The sum of the interior angles of an n-sided polygon is $(n - 2)180°$. For example, in a triangle n = 3, so the sum of the interior angles is $(3 - 2)180° = 180°$. In a quadrilateral, n = 4, and the sum of the angles is $(4 - 2)180° = 360°$. The sum of the interior angles of a polygon is equal to the sum of the interior angles of any other polygon with the same number of sides.

A diagonal is a line segment that joins two non-adjacent vertices of a polygon.
A convex polygon is a polygon whose diagonals all lie within the interior of the polygon.
A concave polygon is a polygon with a least one diagonal that lies outside the polygon. In the diagram below, quadrilateral *ABCD* is concave because diagonal $\overline{AC}$ lies outside the polygon.

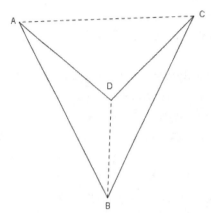

The number of diagonals a polygon has can be found by using the formula: number of diagonals $= \frac{n(n-3)}{2}$, where n is the number of sides in the polygon. This formula works for all polygons, not just regular polygons.

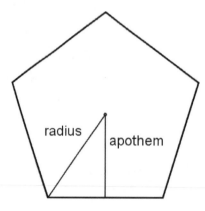

Congruent figures are geometric figures that have the same size and shape. All corresponding angles are equal, and all corresponding sides are equal. It is indicated by the symbol $\cong$.

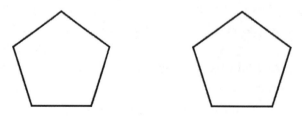

Congruent polygons

Similar figures are geometric figures that have the same shape, but do not necessarily have the same size. All corresponding angles are equal, and all corresponding sides are proportional, but they do not have to be equal. It is indicated by the symbol $\sim$.

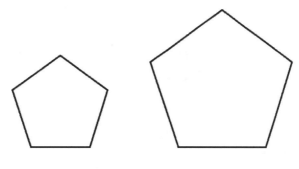

Similar polygons

Note that all congruent figures are also similar, but not all similar figures are congruent.
Line of Symmetry: The line that divides a figure or object into two symmetric parts. Each symmetric half is congruent to the other. An object may have no lines of symmetry, one line of symmetry, or more than one line of symmetry.

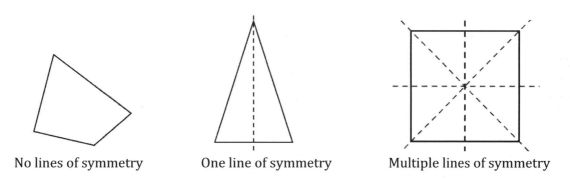

No lines of symmetry   One line of symmetry   Multiple lines of symmetry

Quadrilateral: A closed two-dimensional geometric figure composed of exactly four straight sides. The sum of the interior angles of any quadrilateral is 360°.

Parallelogram: A quadrilateral that has exactly two pairs of opposite parallel sides. The sides that are parallel are also congruent. The opposite interior angles are always congruent, and the consecutive interior angles are supplementary. The diagonals of a parallelogram bisect each other. Each diagonal divides the parallelogram into two congruent triangles.

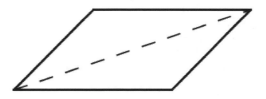

Trapezoid: Traditionally, a quadrilateral that has exactly one pair of parallel sides. Some math texts define trapezoid as a quadrilateral that has at least one pair of parallel sides. Because there are no

rules governing the second pair of sides, there are no rules that apply to the properties of the diagonals of a trapezoid.

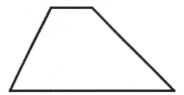

Rectangles, rhombuses, and squares are all special forms of parallelograms.
Rectangle: A parallelogram with four right angles. All rectangles are parallelograms, but not all parallelograms are rectangles. The diagonals of a rectangle are congruent.

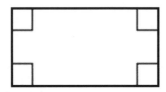

Rhombus: A parallelogram with four congruent sides. All rhombuses are parallelograms, but not all parallelograms are rhombuses. The diagonals of a rhombus are perpendicular to each other.

Square: A parallelogram with four right angles and four congruent sides. All squares are also parallelograms, rhombuses, and rectangles. The diagonals of a square are congruent and perpendicular to each other.

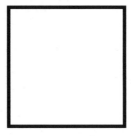

A quadrilateral whose diagonals bisect each other is a parallelogram. A quadrilateral whose opposite sides are parallel (2 pairs of parallel sides) is a parallelogram.

A quadrilateral whose diagonals are perpendicular bisectors of each other is a rhombus. A quadrilateral whose opposite sides (both pairs) are parallel and congruent is a rhombus. A parallelogram that has a right angle is a rectangle. (Consecutive angles of a parallelogram are supplementary. Therefore if there is one right angle in a parallelogram, there are four right angles in that parallelogram.)

A rhombus with one right angle is a square. Because the rhombus is a special form of a parallelogram, the rules about the angles of a parallelogram also apply to the rhombus.

Area and perimeter formulas

The area of a square is found by using the formula $A = s^2$, where and s is the length of one side.

The perimeter of a square is found by using the formula $P = 4s$, where s is the length of one side. Because all four sides are equal in a square, it is faster to multiply the length of one side by 4 than to add the same number four times. You could use the formulas for rectangles and get the same answer.

The area of a rectangle is found by the formula $A = lw$, where A is the area of the rectangle, l is the length (usually considered to be the longer side) and w is the width (usually considered to be the shorter side). The numbers for l and w are interchangeable.
The perimeter of a rectangle is found by the formula $P = 2l + 2w$ or $P = 2(l + w)$, where l is the length, and w is the width. It may be easier to add the length and width first and then double the result, as in the second formula.

The area of a parallelogram is found by the formula $A = bh$, where b is the length of the base, and h is the height. Note that the base and height correspond to the length and width in a rectangle, so this formula would apply to rectangles as well. Do not confuse the height of a parallelogram with the length of the second side. The two are only the same measure in the case of a rectangle.

> ➤ **Review Video: Finding Areas in Geometry**
> Visit **mometrix.com/academy** and enter **Code: 663492**

The perimeter of a parallelogram is found by the formula $P = 2a + 2b$ or $P = 2(a + b)$, where a and b are the lengths of the two sides.

The area of a trapezoid is found by the formula $A = \frac{1}{2}h(b_1 + b_2)$, where h is the height (segment joining and perpendicular to the parallel bases), and b_1 and b_2 are the two parallel sides (bases). Do not use one of the other two sides as the height unless that side is also perpendicular to the parallel bases.

The perimeter of a trapezoid is found by the formula $P = a + b_1 + c + b_2$, where a, b_1, c, and b_2 are the four sides of the trapezoid.

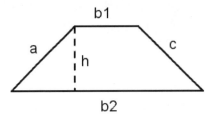

Circles

The center is the single point inside the circle that is equidistant from every point on the circle. (Point O in the diagram below.)

> ➤ **Review Video: Points of a Circle**
> Visit **mometrix.com/academy** and enter **Code: 420746**

The radius is a line segment that joins the center of the circle and any one point on the circle. All radii of a circle are equal. (Segments OX, OY, and OZ in the diagram below.)

The diameter is a line segment that passes through the center of the circle and has both endpoints on the circle. The length of the diameter is exactly twice the length of the radius. (Segment XZ in the diagram below.)

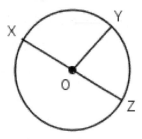

The area of a circle is found by the formula $A = \pi r^2$, where r is the length of the radius. If the diameter of the circle is given, remember to divide it in half to get the length of the radius before proceeding.

The circumference of a circle is found by the formula $C = 2\pi r$, where r is the radius. Again, remember to convert the diameter if you are given that measure rather than the radius.

Concentric circles are circles that have the same center, but not the same length of radii. A bulls-eye target is an example of concentric circles.

An arc is a portion of a circle. Specifically, an arc is the set of points between and including two points on a circle. An arc does not contain any points inside the circle. When a segment is drawn from the endpoints of an arc to the center of the circle, a sector is formed.

A central angle is an angle whose vertex is the center of a circle and whose legs intercept an arc of the circle. Angle *XOY* in the diagram above is a central angle. A minor arc is an arc that has a measure less than 180°. The measure of a central angle is equal to the measure of the minor arc it intercepts. A major arc is an arc having a measure of at least 180°. The measure of the major arc can be found by subtracting the measure of the central angle from 360°.

A semicircle is an arc whose endpoints are the endpoints of the diameter of a circle. A semicircle is exactly half of a circle.

An inscribed angle is an angle whose vertex lies on a circle and whose legs contain chords of that circle. The portion of the circle intercepted by the legs of the angle is called the intercepted arc. The measure of the intercepted arc is exactly twice the measure of the inscribed angle. In the following diagram, angle *ABC* is an inscribed angle. $\widehat{AC} = 2(m\angle ABC)$

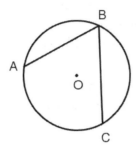

Any angle inscribed in a semicircle is a right angle. The intercepted arc is 180°, making the inscribed angle half that, or 90°. In the diagram below, angle *ABC* is inscribed in semicircle *ABC*, making angle *ABC* equal to 90°.

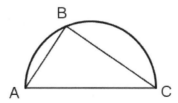

A chord is a line segment that has both endpoints on a circle. In the diagram below, $\overline{EB}$ is a chord. Secant: A line that passes through a circle and contains a chord of that circle. In the diagram below, $\overleftrightarrow{EB}$ is a secant and contains chord $\overline{EB}$.

A tangent is a line in the same plane as a circle that touches the circle in exactly one point. While a line segment can be tangent to a circle as part of a line that is tangent, it is improper to say a tangent can be simply a line segment that touches the circle in exactly one point. In the diagram below, $\overleftrightarrow{CD}$ is tangent to circle A. Notice that $\overline{FB}$ is not tangent to the circle. $\overline{FB}$ is a line segment that touches the circle in exactly one point, but if the segment were extended, it would touch the circle in a second point. The point at which a tangent touches a circle is called the point of tangency. In the diagram below, point B is the point of tangency.

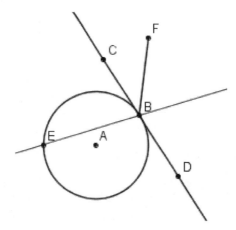

A secant is a line that intersects a circle in two points. Two secants may intersect inside the circle, on the circle, or outside the circle. When the two secants intersect on the circle, an inscribed angle is formed.

When two secants intersect inside a circle, the measure of each of two vertical angles is equal to half the sum of the two intercepted arcs. In the diagram below, $m\angle AEB = \frac{1}{2}(\widehat{AB} + \widehat{CD})$ and $m\angle BEC = \frac{1}{2}(\widehat{BC} + \widehat{AD})$.

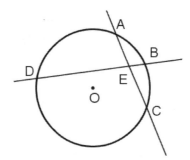

When two secants intersect outside a circle, the measure of the angle formed is equal to half the difference of the two arcs that lie between the two secants. In the diagram below, $m\angle E = \frac{1}{2}(\widehat{AB} - \widehat{CD})$.

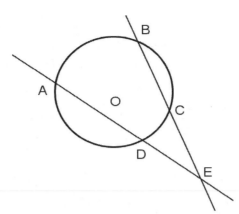

The arc length is the length of that portion of the circumference between two points on the circle. The formula for arc length is $s = \frac{\pi r \theta}{180°}$ where s is the arc length, r is the length of the radius, and θ is the angular measure of the arc in degrees, or $s = r\theta$, where θ is the angular measure of the arc in radians (2π radians = 360 degrees).

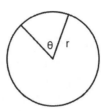

A sector is the portion of a circle formed by two radii and their intercepted arc. While the arc length is exclusively the points that are also on the circumference of the circle, the sector is the entire area bounded by the arc and the two radii.

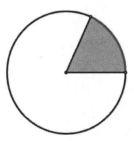

The area of a sector of a circle is found by the formula, $A = \frac{\theta r^2}{2}$, where A is the area, θ is the measure of the central angle in radians, and r is the radius. To find the area when the central angle is in degrees, use the formula, $A = \frac{\theta \pi r^2}{360}$, where θ is the measure of the central angle in degrees and r is the radius.

A circle is inscribed in a polygon if each of the sides of the polygon is tangent to the circle. A polygon is inscribed in a circle if each of the vertices of the polygon lies on the circle.

A circle is circumscribed about a polygon if each of the vertices of the polygon lies on the circle. A polygon is circumscribed about the circle if each of the sides of the polygon is tangent to the circle.

If one figure is inscribed in another, then the other figure is circumscribed about the first figure.

Circle circumscribed about a pentagon
Pentagon inscribed in a circle

Other conic sections

An ellipse is the set of all points in a plane, whose total distance from two fixed points called the foci (singular: focus) is constant, and whose center is the midpoint between the foci.

The standard equation of an ellipse that is taller than it is wide is $\frac{(y-k)^2}{a^2} + \frac{(x-h)^2}{b^2} = 1$, where a and b are coefficients. The center is the point (h, k) and the foci are the points $(h, k + c)$ and $(h, k - c)$, where $c^2 = a^2 - b^2$ and $a^2 > b^2$.

The major axis has length $2a$, and the minor axis has length $2b$.

Eccentricity (e) is a measure of how elongated an ellipse is, and is the ratio of the distance between the foci to the length of the major axis. Eccentricity will have a value between 0 and 1. The closer to 1 the eccentricity is, the closer the ellipse is to being a circle. The formula for eccentricity is $= \frac{c}{a}$.

Parabola: The set of all points in a plane that are equidistant from a fixed line, called the directrix, and a fixed point not on the line, called the focus.

Axis: The line perpendicular to the directrix that passes through the focus.

For parabolas that open up or down, the standard equation is $(x - h)^2 = 4c(y - k)$, where h, c, and k are coefficients. If c is positive, the parabola opens up. If c is negative, the parabola opens down. The vertex is the point (h, k). The directrix is the line having the equation $y = -c + k$, and the focus is the point $(h, c + k)$.

For parabolas that open left or right, the standard equation is $(y - k)^2 = 4c(x - h)$, where k, c, and h are coefficients. If c is positive, the parabola opens to the right. If c is negative, the parabola opens to the left. The vertex is the point (h, k). The directrix is the line having the equation $x = -c + h$, and the focus is the point $(c + h, k)$.

A hyperbola is the set of all points in a plane, whose distance from two fixed points, called foci, has a constant difference.

The standard equation of a horizontal hyperbola is $\frac{(x-h)^2}{a^2} - \frac{(y-k)^2}{b^2} = 1$, where a, b, h, and k are real numbers. The center is the point (h, k), the vertices are the points $(h + a, k)$ and $(h - a, k)$, and the foci are the points that every point on one of the parabolic curves is equidistant from and are found using the formulas $(h + c, k)$ and $(h - c, k)$, where $c^2 = a^2 + b^2$. The asymptotes are two lines the graph of the hyperbola approaches but never reaches, and are given by the equations $y = \left(\frac{b}{a}\right)(x - h) + k$ and $y = -\left(\frac{b}{a}\right)(x - h) + k$.

A vertical hyperbola is formed when a plane makes a vertical cut through two cones that are stacked vertex-to-vertex.

The standard equation of a vertical hyperbola is $\frac{(y-k)^2}{a^2} - \frac{(x-h)^2}{b^2} = 1$, where a, b, k, and h are real numbers. The center is the point (h, k), the vertices are the points $(h, k + a)$ and $(h, k - a)$, and the foci are the points that every point on one of the parabolic curves is equidistant from and are found using the formulas $(h, k + c)$ and $(h, k - c)$, where $c^2 = a^2 + b^2$. The asymptotes are two lines the graph of the hyperbola approaches but never reach, and are given by the equations $y = \left(\frac{a}{b}\right)(x - h) + k$ and $y = -\left(\frac{a}{b}\right)(x - h) + k$.

Solids
The surface area of a solid object is the area of all sides or exterior surfaces. For objects such as prisms and pyramids, a further distinction is made between base surface area (B) and lateral surface area (LA). For a prism, the total surface area (SA) is $SA = LA + 2B$. For a pyramid or cone, the total surface area is $SA = LA + B$.

The surface area of a sphere can be found by the formula $A = 4\pi r^2$, where r is the radius. The volume is given by the formula $V = \frac{4}{3}\pi r^3$, where r is the radius. Both quantities are generally given in terms of π.

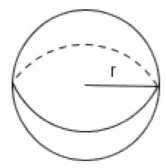

The volume of any prism is found by the formula $V = Bh$, where B is the area of the base, and h is the height (perpendicular distance between the bases). The surface area of any prism is the sum of the areas of both bases and all sides. It can be calculated as $SA = 2B + Ph$, where P is the perimeter of the base.

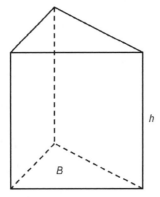

For a rectangular prism, the volume can be found by the formula $V = lwh$, where V is the volume, l is the length, w is the width, and h is the height. The surface area can be calculated as $SA = 2lw + 2hl + 2wh$ or $SA = 2(lw + hl + wh)$.

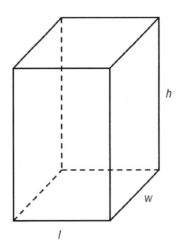

The volume of a cube can be found by the formula $V = s^3$, where s is the length of a side. The surface area of a cube is calculated as $SA = 6s^2$, where SA is the total surface area and s is the length of a side. These formulas are the same as the ones used for the volume and surface area of a rectangular prism, but simplified since all three quantities (length, width, and height) are the same.

The volume of a cylinder can be calculated by the formula $V = \pi r^2 h$, where r is the radius, and h is the height. The surface area of a cylinder can be found by the formula $SA = 2\pi r^2 + 2\pi rh$. The first term is the base area multiplied by two, and the second term is the perimeter of the base multiplied by the height.

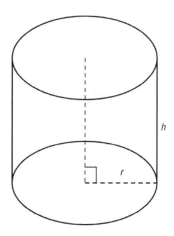

The volume of a pyramid is found by the formula $V = \frac{1}{3}Bh$, where B is the area of the base, and h is the height (perpendicular distance from the vertex to the base). Notice this formula is the same as $\frac{1}{3}$ times the volume of a prism. Like a prism, the base of a pyramid can be any shape. Finding the surface area of a pyramid is not as simple as the other shapes we've looked at thus far. If the pyramid is a right pyramid, meaning the base is a regular polygon and the vertex is directly over the center of that polygon, the surface area can be calculated as $SA = B + \frac{1}{2}Ph_s$, where P is the perimeter of the base, and h_s is the slant height (distance from the vertex to the midpoint of one side of the base). If the pyramid is irregular, the area of each triangle side must be calculated individually and then summed, along with the base.

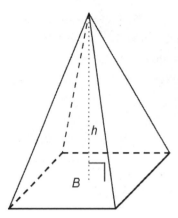

The volume of a cone is found by the formula $V = \frac{1}{3}\pi r^2 h$, where r is the radius, and h is the height. Notice this is the same as $\frac{1}{3}$ times the volume of a cylinder. The surface area can be calculated as $SA = \pi r^2 + \pi rs$, where s is the slant height. The slant height can be calculated using the Pythagorean Thereom to be $\sqrt{r^2 + h^2}$, so the surface area formula can also be written as $SA = \pi r^2 + \pi r\sqrt{r^2 + h^2}$.

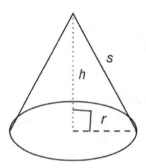

➤ **Review Video: <u>Finding Volume in Geometry</u>**
*Visit **mometrix.com/academy** and enter **Code: 754774***

Trigonometry

Basic Trigonometric Functions

The three basic trigonometric functions are sine, cosine, and tangent.

Sine

The sine (sin) function has a period of $360°$ or 2π radians. This means that its graph makes one complete cycle every $360°$ or 2π. Because $\sin 0 = 0$, the graph of $y = \sin x$ begins at the origin, with the x-axis representing the angle measure, and the y-axis representing the sine of the angle. The graph of the sine function is a smooth curve that begins at the origin, peaks at the point $\left(\frac{\pi}{2}, 1\right)$, crosses the x-axis at $(\pi, 0)$, has its lowest point at $\left(\frac{3\pi}{2}, -1\right)$, and returns to the x-axis to complete one cycle at $(2\pi, 0)$.

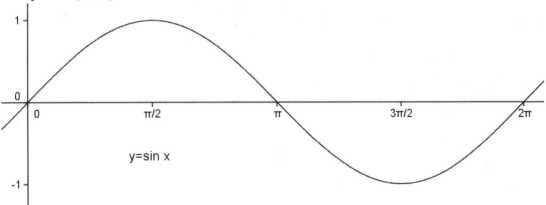

Cosine

The cosine (cos) function also has a period of $360°$ or 2π radians, which means that its graph also makes one complete cycle every $360°$ or 2π. Because $\cos 0° = 1$, the graph of $y = \cos x$ begins at the point $(0, 1)$, with the x-axis representing the angle measure, and the y-axis representing the cosine of the angle. The graph of the cosine function is a smooth curve that begins at the point $(0, 1)$, crosses the x-axis at the point $\left(\frac{\pi}{2}, 0\right)$, has its lowest point at $(\pi, -1)$, crosses the x-axis again at the point $\left(\frac{3\pi}{2}, 0\right)$, and returns to a peak at the point $(2\pi, 1)$ to complete one cycle.

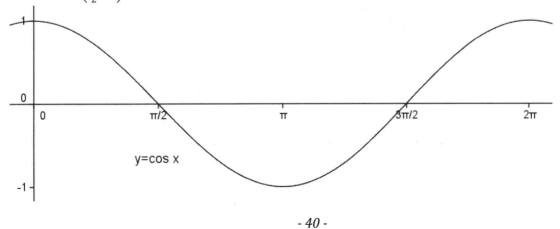

Tangent

The tangent (tan) function has a period of 180° or π radians, which means that its graph makes one complete cycle every 180° or π radians. The x-axis represents the angle measure, and the y-axis represents the tangent of the angle. The graph of the tangent function is a series of smooth curves that cross the x-axis at every 180° or π radians and have an asymptote every $k \cdot 90°$ or $\frac{k\pi}{2}$ radians, where k is an odd integer. This can be explained by the fact that the tangent is calculated by dividing the sine by the cosine, since the cosine equals zero at those asymptote points.

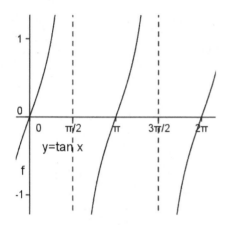

> ➤ **Review Video: Finding Tangent**
> Visit *mometrix.com/academy* and enter *Code: 947639*

Defined and Reciprocal Functions

The tangent function is defined as the ratio of the sine to the cosine:

Tangent (tan):

$$\tan x = \frac{\sin x}{\cos x}$$

To take the reciprocal of a number means to place that number as the denominator of a fraction with a numerator of 1. The reciprocal functions are thus defined quite simply.

Cosecant (csc):

$$\csc x = \frac{1}{\sin x}$$

Secant (sec):

$$\sec x = \frac{1}{\cos x}$$

Cotangent (cot):

$$\cot x = \frac{1}{\tan x}$$

- 41 -

It is important to know these reciprocal functions, but they are not as commonly used as the three basic functions.

Inverse Functions

Each of the trigonometric functions accepts an angular measure, either degrees or radians, and gives a numerical value as the output. The inverse functions do the opposite; they accept a numerical value and give an angular measure as the output. The inverse sine, or arcsine, commonly written as either $\sin^{-1} x$ or $\arcsin x$, gives the angle whose sine is x. Similarly:

The inverse of $\cos x$ is written as $\cos^{-1} x$ or $\arccos x$ and means the angle whose cosine is x.
The inverse of $\tan x$ is written as $\tan^{-1} x$ or $\arctan x$ and means the angle whose tangent is x.
The inverse of $\csc x$ is written as $\csc^{-1} x$ or $\text{arccsc}\, x$ and means the angle whose cosecant is x.
The inverse of $\sec x$ is written as $\sec^{-1} x$ or $\text{arcsec}\, x$ and means the angle whose secant is x.
The inverse of $\cot x$ is written as $\cot^{-1} x$ or $\text{arccot}\, x$ and means the angle whose cotangent is x.

Important note about solving trigonometric equations
Trigonometric and algebraic equations are solved following the same rules, but while algebraic expressions have one unique solution, trigonometric equations could have multiple solutions, and you must find them all. When solving for an angle with a known trigonometric value, you must consider the sign and include all angles with that value. Your calculator will probably only give one value as an answer, typically in the following ranges:
For the inverse sine function, $\left[-\frac{\pi}{2}, \frac{\pi}{2}\right]$ or $[-90°, 90°]$
For the inverse cosine function, $[0, \pi]$ or $[0°, 180°]$
For the inverse tangent function, $\left[-\frac{\pi}{2}, \frac{\pi}{2}\right]$ or $[-90°, 90°]$

It is important to determine if there is another angle in a different quadrant that also satisfies the problem. To do this, find the other quadrant(s) with the same sign for that trigonometric function and find the angle that has the same reference angle. Then check whether this angle is also a solution.

In the first quadrant, all six trigonometric functions are positive (sin, cos, tan, csc, sec, cot).
In the second quadrant, sin and csc are positive.
In the third quadrant, tan and cot are positive.
In the fourth quadrant, cos and sec are positive.
If you remember the phrase, "ALL Students Take Classes," you will be able to remember the sign of each trigonometric function in each quadrant. ALL represents all the signs in the first quadrant. The "S" in "Students" represents the sine function and its reciprocal in the second quadrant. The "T" in "Take" represents the tangent function and its reciprocal in the third quadrant. The "C" in "Classes" represents the cosine function and its reciprocal.

Trigonometric Identities

<u>Sum and Difference</u>

To find the sine, cosine, or tangent of the sum or difference of two angles, use one of the following formulas:

$$\sin(\alpha \pm \beta) = \sin \alpha \cos \beta \pm \cos \alpha \sin \beta$$
$$\cos(\alpha \pm \beta) = \cos \alpha \cos \beta \mp \sin \alpha \sin \beta$$
$$\tan(\alpha \pm \beta) = \frac{\tan \alpha \pm \tan \beta}{1 \mp \tan \alpha \tan \beta}$$

where α and β are two angles with known sine, cosine, or tangent values as needed.

<u>Half angle</u>

To find the sine or cosine of half of a known angle, use the following formulas:

$$\sin \frac{\theta}{2} = \pm \sqrt{\frac{1 - \cos \theta}{2}}$$

$$\cos \frac{\theta}{2} = \pm \sqrt{\frac{1 + \cos \theta}{2}}$$

where θ is an angle with a known exact cosine value.

To determine the sign of the answer, you must notice the quadrant the given angle is in and apply the correct sign for the trigonometric function you are using. If you need to find the exact sine or cosine of an angle that you do not know, such as $\sin 22.5°$, you can rewrite the given angle as a half angle, such as $\sin \frac{45°}{2}$, and use the formula above.

To find the tangent or cotangent of half of a known angle, use the following formulas:

$$\tan \frac{\theta}{2} = \frac{\sin \theta}{1 + \cos \theta}$$
$$\cot \frac{\theta}{2} = \frac{\sin \theta}{1 - \cos \theta}$$

where θ is an angle with known exact sine and cosine values.

These formulas will work for finding the tangent or cotangent of half of any angle unless the cosine of θ happens to make the denominator of the identity equal to 0.

<u>Double angles</u>

In each case, use one of the Double Angle Formulas.

- 43 -

To find the sine or cosine of twice a known angle, use one of the following formulas:

$$\sin(2\theta) = 2\sin\theta\cos\theta$$
$$\cos(2\theta) = \cos^2\theta - \sin^2\theta \ \text{ or}$$
$$\cos(2\theta) = 2\cos^2\theta - 1 \ \text{ or}$$
$$\cos(2\theta) = 1 - 2\sin^2\theta$$

To find the tangent or cotangent of twice a known angle, use the formulas:

$$\tan(2\theta) = \frac{2\tan\theta}{1-\tan^2\theta}$$
$$\cot(2\theta) = \frac{\cot\theta - \tan\theta}{2}$$

In each case, θ is an angle with known exact sine, cosine, tangent, and cotangent values.

Products

To find the product of the sines and cosines of two different angles, use one of the following formulas:

$$\sin\alpha\sin\beta = \frac{1}{2}[\cos(\alpha-\beta) - \cos(\alpha+\beta)]$$
$$\cos\alpha\cos\beta = \frac{1}{2}[\cos(\alpha+\beta) + \cos(\alpha-\beta)]$$
$$\sin\alpha\cos\beta = \frac{1}{2}[\sin(\alpha+\beta) + \sin(\alpha-\beta)]$$
$$\cos\alpha\sin\beta = \frac{1}{2}[\sin(\alpha+\beta) - \sin(\alpha-\beta)]$$

where α and β are two unique angles.

Complementary

The trigonometric cofunction identities use the trigonometric relationships of complementary angles (angles whose sum is 90°). These are:

$$\cos x = \sin(90° - x)$$
$$\csc x = \sec(90° - x)$$
$$\cot x = \tan(90° - x)$$

Pythagorean

The Pythagorean Theorem states that $a^2 + b^2 = c^2$ for all right triangles. The trigonometric identity that derives from this principles is stated in this way:

$$\sin^2\theta + \cos^2\theta = 1$$

Dividing each term by either $\sin^2\theta$ or $\cos^2\theta$ yields two other identities, respectively:

$$1 + \cot^2\theta = \csc^2\theta$$
$$\tan^2\theta + 1 = \sec^2\theta$$

> ➤ **Review Video: Pythagorean Theorem**
> *Visit **mometrix.com/academy** and enter **Code: 906576***

Unit Circle

A unit circle is a circle with a radius of 1 that has its center at the origin. The equation of the unit circle is $x^2 + y^2 = 1$. Notice that this is an abbreviated version of the standard equation of a circle. Because the center is the point $(0, 0)$, the values of h and k in the general equation are equal to zero and the equation simplifies to this form.

Standard Position is the position of an angle of measure θ whose vertex is at the origin, the initial side crosses the unit circle at the point $(1, 0)$, and the terminal side crosses the unit circle at some other point (a, b). In the standard position, $\sin \theta = b$, $\cos \theta = a$, and $\tan \theta = \frac{b}{a}$.

Rectangular coordinates are those that lie on the square grids of the Cartesian plane. They should be quite familiar to you. The polar coordinate system is based on a circular graph, rather than the square grid of the Cartesian system. Points in the polar coordinate system are in the format (r, θ), where r is the distance from the origin (think radius of the circle) and θ is the smallest positive angle (moving counterclockwise around the circle) made with the positive horizontal axis.

To convert a point from rectangular (x, y) format to polar (r, θ) format, use the formula
(x, y) to $(r, \theta) \Rightarrow r = \sqrt{x^2 + y^2}; \theta = \arctan \frac{y}{x}$ when $x \neq 0$
If x is positive, use the positive square root value for r. If x is negative, use the negative square root value for r.
If x = 0, use the following rules:
If x = 0 and y = 0, then $\theta = 0$
If x = 0 and y > 0, then $\theta = \frac{\pi}{2}$
If x = 0 and y < 0, then $\theta = \frac{3\pi}{2}$
To convert a point from polar (r, θ) format to rectangular (x, y) format, use the formula
(r, θ) to $(x, y) \Rightarrow x = r \cos \theta ; y = r \sin \theta$

Table of commonly encountered angles
$0° = 0$ radians, $30° = \frac{\pi}{6}$ radians, $45° = \frac{\pi}{4}$ radians, $60° = \frac{\pi}{3}$ radians, and $90° = \frac{\pi}{2}$ radians

$\sin 0° = 0$	$\cos 0° = 1$	$\tan 0° = 0$
$\sin 30° = \frac{1}{2}$	$\cos 30° = \frac{\sqrt{3}}{2}$	$\tan 30° = \frac{\sqrt{3}}{3}$
$\sin 45° = \frac{\sqrt{2}}{2}$	$\cos 45° = \frac{\sqrt{2}}{2}$	$\tan 45° = 1$
$\sin 60° = \frac{\sqrt{3}}{2}$	$\cos 60° = \frac{1}{2}$	$\tan 60° = \sqrt{3}$
$\sin 90° = 1$	$\cos 90° = 0$	$\tan 90° = $ undefined
$\csc 0° = $ undefined	$\sec 0° = 1$	$\cot 0° = $ undefined

$\csc 30° = 2$	$\sec 30° = \dfrac{2\sqrt{3}}{3}$	$\cot 30° = \sqrt{3}$
$\csc 45° = \sqrt{2}$	$\sec 45° = \sqrt{2}$	$\cot 45° = 1$
$\csc 60° = \dfrac{2\sqrt{3}}{3}$	$\sec 60° = 2$	$\cot 60° = \dfrac{\sqrt{3}}{3}$
$\csc 90° = 1$	$\sec 90° = $ undefined	$\cot 90° = 0$

The values in the upper half of this table are values you should have memorized or be able to find quickly.

College Math

Functions

A function is an equation that has exactly one value of output variable (dependent variable) for each value of the input variable (independent variable). The set of all values for the input variable (here assumed to be x) is the domain of the function, and the set of all corresponding values of output variable (here assumed to be y) is the range of the function. When looking at a graph of an equation, the easiest way to determine if the equation is a function or not is to conduct the vertical line test. If a vertical line drawn through any value of x crosses the graph in more than one place, the equation is not a function.

In functions with the notation $f(x)$, the value substituted for x in the equation is called the argument. The domain is the set of all values for x in a function. Unless otherwise given, assume the domain is the set of real numbers that will yield real numbers for the range. This is the domain of definition. The graph of a function is the set of all ordered pairs (x, y) that satisfy the equation of the function. The points that have zero as the value for y are called the zeros of the function. These are also the x-intercepts, because that is the point at which the graph crosses, or intercepts, the x-axis. The points that have zero as the value for x are the y-intercepts because that is where the graph crosses the y-axis.

> ➤ **Review Video:** <u>Basics of Functions</u>
> *Visit* **mometrix.com/academy** *and enter* **Code: 822500**

Any time there are vertical asymptotes or holes in a graph, such that the complete graph cannot be drawn as one continuous line, a graph is said to have discontinuities. Examples would include the graphs of hyperbolas that are functions, and the function $f(x) = \tan x$.

Manipulation of Functions

Horizontal and vertical shift occur when values are added to or subtracted from the x or y values, respectively.

If a constant is added to the y portion of each point, the graph shifts up. If a constant is subtracted from the y portion of each point, the graph shifts down. This is represented by the expression $f(x) \pm k$, where k is a constant.

If a constant is added to the x portion of each point, the graph shifts left. If a constant is subtracted from the x portion of each point, the graph shifts right. This is represented by the expression $f(x \pm k)$, where k is a constant.

Stretch, compression, and reflection occur when different parts of a function are multiplied by different groups of constants. If the function as a whole is multiplied by a real number constant greater than 1 ($k \times f(x)$), the graph is stretched vertically. If k in the previous equation is greater than zero but less than 1, the graph is compressed vertically. If k is less than zero, the graph is reflected about the x-axis, in addition to being either stretched or compressed vertically if k is less than or greater than -1, respectively. If instead, just the x-term is multiplied by a constant greater than 1 ($f(k \times x)$), the graph is compressed horizontally. If k in the previous equation is greater than zero but less than 1, the graph is stretched horizontally. If k is less than zero, the graph is reflected about the y-axis, in addition to being either stretched or compressed horizontally if k is greater than or less than -1, respectively.

Classification of Functions

There are many different ways to classify functions based on their structure or behavior. Listed here are a few common classifications.

Constant functions are given by the equation $y = b$ or $f(x) = b$, where b is a real number. There is no independent variable present in the equation, so the function has a constant value for all x. The graph of a constant function is a horizontal line of slope 0 that is positioned b units from the x-axis. If b is positive, the line is above the x-axis; if b is negative, the line is below the x-axis.

Identity functions are identified by the equation $y = x$ or $f(x) = x$, where every value of y is equal to its corresponding value of x. The only zero is the point $(0, 0)$. The graph is a diagonal line with slope 1.

In **linear functions**, the value of the function changes in direct proportion to x. The rate of change, represented by the slope on its graph, is constant throughout. The standard form of a linear equation is $ax + by = c$, where a, b, and c are real numbers. As a function, this equation is commonly written as $y = mx + b$ or $f(x) = mx + b$. This is known as the slope-intercept form, because the coefficients give the slope of the graphed function (m) and its y-intercept (b). Solve the equation $mx + b = 0$ for x to get $x = -\frac{b}{m}$, which is the only zero of the function. The domain and range are both the set of all real numbers.

A **polynomial function** is a function with multiple terms and multiple powers of x, such as
$$f(x) = a_n x^n + a_{n-1} x^{n-1} + a_{n-2} x^{n-2} + \cdots + a_1 x + a_0$$
where n is a non-negative integer that is the highest exponent in the polynomial, and $a_n \neq 0$. The domain of a polynomial function is the set of all real numbers. If the greatest exponent in the polynomial is even, the polynomial is said to be of even degree and the range is the set of real

numbers that satisfy the function. If the greatest exponent in the polynomial is odd, the polynomial is said to be odd and the range, like the domain, is the set of all real numbers.

A **quadratic function** is a polynomial function that follows the equation pattern $y = ax^2 + bx + c$, or $f(x) = ax^2 + bx + c$, where a, b, and c are real numbers and $a \neq 0$. The domain of a quadratic function is the set of all real numbers. The range is also real numbers, but only those in the subset of the domain that satisfy the equation. The root(s) of any quadratic function can be found by plugging the values of a, b, and c into the **quadratic formula**:

$$x = \frac{-b \pm \sqrt{b^2 - 4ac}}{2a}$$

If the expression $b^2 - 4ac$ is negative, you will instead find complex roots.
A quadratic function has a parabola for its graph. In the equation $f(x) = ax^2 + bx + c$, if a is positive, the parabola will open upward. If a is negative, the parabola will open downward. The axis of symmetry is a vertical line that passes through the vertex. To determine whether or not the parabola will intersect the x-axis, check the number of real roots. An equation with two real roots will cross the x-axis twice. An equation with one real root will have its vertex on the x-axis. An equation with no real roots will not contact the x-axis.

A **rational function** is a function that can be constructed as a ratio of two polynomial expressions: $f(x) = \frac{p(x)}{q(x)}$, where $p(x)$ and $q(x)$ are both polynomial expressions and $q(x) \neq 0$. The domain is the set of all real numbers, except any values for which $q(x) = 0$. The range is the set of real numbers that satisfies the function when the domain is applied. When you graph a rational function, you will have vertical asymptotes wherever $q(x) = 0$. If the polynomial in the numerator is of lesser degree than the polynomial in the denominator, the x-axis will also be a horizontal asymptote. If the numerator and denominator have equal degrees, there will be a horizontal asymptote not on the x-axis. If the degree of the numerator is exactly one greater than the degree of the denominator, the graph will have an oblique, or diagonal, asymptote. The asymptote will be along the line $y = \frac{p_n}{q_{n-1}} x + \frac{p_{n-1}}{q_{n-1}}$, where p_n and q_{n-1} are the coefficients of the highest degree terms in their respective polynomials.

A **square root function** is a function that contains a radical and is in the format $f(x) = \sqrt{ax + b}$. The domain is the set of all real numbers that yields a positive radicand or a radicand equal to zero. Because square root values are assumed to be positive unless otherwise identified, the range is all real numbers from zero to infinity. To find the zero of a square root function, set the radicand equal to zero and solve for x. The graph of a square root function is always to the right of the zero and always above the x-axis.

An **absolute value function** is in the format $f(x) = |ax + b|$. Like other functions, the domain is the set of all real numbers. However, because absolute value indicates positive numbers, the range is limited to positive real numbers. To find the zero of an absolute value function, set the portion inside the absolute value sign equal to zero and solve for x. An absolute value function is also known as a piecewise function because it must be solved in pieces – one for if the value inside the absolute value sign is positive, and one for if the value is negative. The function can be expressed as

$$f(x) = \begin{cases} ax + b & \text{if } ax + b \geq 0 \\ -(ax + b) & \text{if } ax + b < 0 \end{cases}$$

This will allow for an accurate statement of the range.

Exponential functions are equations that have the format $y = b^x$, where base $b > 0$ and $b \neq 1$. The exponential function can also be written $f(x) = b^x$. **Logarithmic functions** are equations that have the format $y = \log_b x$ or $f(x) = \log_b x$. The base b may be any number except one; however, the most common bases for logarithms are base 10 and base e. The log base e is known the natural logarithm, or ln, expressed by the function $f(x) = \ln x$. Any logarithm that does not have an assigned value of b is assumed to be base 10: $\log x = \log_{10} x$. Exponential functions and logarithmic functions are related in that one is the inverse of the other. If $f(x) = b^x$, then $f^{-1}(x) = \log_b x$. This can perhaps be expressed more clearly by the two equations: $y = b^x$ and $x = \log_b y$.
The following properties apply to logarithmic expressions:

$$\log_b 1 = 0$$
$$\log_b b = 1$$
$$\log_b b^p = p$$
$$\log_b MN = \log_b M + \log_b N$$
$$\log_b \frac{M}{N} = \log_b M - \log_b N$$
$$\log_b M^p = p \log_b M$$

In a **one-to-one function**, each value of x has exactly one value for y (this is the definition of a function) *and* each value of y has exactly one value for x. While the vertical line test will determine if a graph is that of a function, the horizontal line test will determine if a function is a one-to-one function. If a horizontal line drawn at any value of y intersects the graph in more than one place, the graph is not that of a one-to-one function. Do not make the mistake of using the horizontal line test exclusively in determining if a graph is that of a one-to-one function. A one-to-one function must pass both the vertical line test and the horizontal line test. One-to-one functions are also **invertible functions**.

A **monotone function** is a function whose graph either constantly increases or constantly decreases. Examples include the functions $f(x) = x$, $f(x) = -x$, or $f(x) = x^3$.
An **even function** has a graph that is symmetric with respect to the y-axis and satisfies the equation $f(x) = f(-x)$. Examples include the functions $f(x) = x^2$ and $f(x) = ax^n$, where a is any real number and n is a positive even integer.
An **odd function** has a graph that is symmetric with respect to the origin and satisfies the equation $f(x) = -f(-x)$. Examples include the functions $f(x) = x^3$ and $f(x) = ax^n$, where a is any real number and n is a positive odd integer.

Algebraic functions are those that exclusively use polynomials and roots. These would include polynomial functions, rational functions, square root functions, and all combinations of these functions, such as polynomials as the radicand. These combinations may be joined by addition, subtraction, multiplication, or division, but may not include variables as exponents. **Transcendental functions** are all functions that are non-algebraic. Any function that includes logarithms, trigonometric functions, variables as exponents, or any combination that includes any of these is not algebraic in nature, even if the function includes polynomials or roots.

Related concepts

According to the **Fundamental Theorem of Algebra**, every non-constant, single variable polynomial has exactly as many roots as the polynomial's highest exponent. For example, if x^4 is the largest exponent of a term, the polynomial will have exactly 4 roots. However, some of these roots may have multiplicity or be non-real numbers. For instance, in the polynomial function $f(x) = x^4 - 4x + 3$, the only real roots are 1 and -1. The root 1 has multiplicity of 2 and there is one non-real root $(-1 - \sqrt{2}i)$.

The **Remainder Theorem** is useful for determining the remainder when a polynomial is divided by a binomial. The Remainder Theorem states that if a polynomial function $f(x)$ is divided by a binomial $x - a$, where a is a real number, the remainder of the division will be the value of $f(a)$. If $f(a)$ = 0, then a is a root of the polynomial.

The **Factor Theorem** is related to the Remainder Theorem and states that if $f(a)$ = 0 then $(x - a)$ is a factor of the function.

According to the **Rational Root Theorem,** any rational root of a polynomial function $f(x) = a_n x^n + a_{n-1} x^{n-1} + \cdots + a_1 x + a_0$ with integer coefficients will, when reduced to its lowest terms, be a positive or negative fraction such that the numerator is a factor of a_0 and the denominator is a factor of a_n. For instance, if the polynomial function $f(x) = x^3 + 3x^2 - 4$ has any rational roots, the numerators of those roots can only be factors of 4 (1, 2, 4), and the denominators can only be factors of 1 (1). The function in this example has roots of 1 (or $\frac{1}{1}$) and -2 (or $-\frac{2}{1}$).

Variables that vary directly are those that either both increase at the same rate or both decrease at the same rate. For example, in the functions $f(x) = kx$ or $f(x) = kx^n$, where k and n are positive, the value of $f(x)$ increases as the value of x increases and decreases as the value of x decreases.

Variables that vary inversely are those where one increases while the other decreases. For example, in the functions $f(x) = \frac{k}{x}$ or $f(x) = \frac{k}{x^n}$ where k is a positive constant, the value of y increases as the value of x decreases, and the value of y decreases as the value of x increases. In both cases, k is the constant of variation.

Applying the Basic Operations to Functions

For each of the basic operations, we will use these functions as examples: $f(x) = x^2$ and $g(x) = x$. To find the sum of two functions f and g, assuming the domains are compatible, simply add the two functions together: $(f + g)(x) = f(x) + g(x) = x^2 + x$

To find the difference of two functions f and g, assuming the domains are compatible, simply subtract the second function from the first: $(f - g)(x) = f(x) - g(x) = x^2 - x$.

To find the product of two functions f and g, assuming the domains are compatible, multiply the two functions together: $(f \cdot g)(x) = f(x) \cdot g(x) = x^2 \cdot x = x^3$.

To find the quotient of two functions f and g, assuming the domains are compatible, divide the first function by the second: $\frac{f}{g}(x) = \frac{f(x)}{g(x)} = \frac{x^2}{x} = x \; ; x \neq 0$.

The example given in each case is fairly simple, but on a given problem, if you are looking only for the value of the sum, difference, product or quotient of two functions at a particular x-value, it may be simpler to solve the functions individually and then perform the given operation using those values.

The composite of two functions f and g, written as $(f \circ g)(x)$ simply means that the output of the second function is used as the input of the first. This can also be written as $f(g(x))$. In general, this can be solved by substituting $g(x)$ for all instances of x in $f(x)$ and simplifying. Using the example functions $f(x) = x^2 - x + 2$ and $g(x) = x + 1$, we can find that $(f \circ g)(x)$ or $f(g(x))$ is equal to $f(x + 1) = (x + 1)^2 - (x + 1) + 2$, which simplifies to $x^2 + x + 2$.

It is important to note that $(f \circ g)(x)$ is not necessarily the same as $(g \circ f)(x)$. The process is not commutative like addition or multiplication expressions. If $(f \circ g)(x)$ does equal $(g \circ f)(x)$, the two functions are inverses of each other.

Matrix Algebra

Matrix Basics

A **matrix** (plural: matrices) is a rectangular array of numbers or variables, often called **elements**, which are arranged in columns and rows. A matrix is generally represented by a capital letter, with its elements represented by the corresponding lowercase letter with two subscripts indicating the row and column of the element. For example, n_{ab} represents the element in row a column b of matrix N.

$$N = \begin{bmatrix} n_{11} & n_{12} & n_{13} \\ n_{21} & n_{22} & n_{23} \end{bmatrix}$$

A matrix can be described in terms of the number of rows and columns it contains in the format $a \times b$, where a is the number of rows and b is the number of columns. The matrix shown above is a 2×3 matrix. Any $a \times b$ matrix where $a = b$ is a square matrix. A **vector** is a matrix that has exactly one column (**column vector**) or exactly one row (**row vector**).

The **main diagonal** of a matrix is the set of elements on the diagonal from the top left to the bottom right of a matrix. Because of the way it is defined, only square matrices will have a main diagonal. For the matrix shown below, the main diagonal consists of the elements $n_{11}, n_{22}, n_{33}, n_{44}$.

$$\begin{bmatrix} n_{11} & n_{12} & n_{13} & n_{14} \\ n_{21} & n_{22} & n_{23} & n_{24} \\ n_{31} & n_{32} & n_{33} & n_{34} \\ n_{41} & n_{42} & n_{43} & n_{44} \end{bmatrix}$$

A 3×4 matrix such as the one shown below would not have a main diagonal because there is no straight line of elements between the top left corner and the bottom right corner that joins the elements.

$$\begin{bmatrix} n_{11} & n_{12} & n_{13} & n_{14} \\ n_{21} & n_{22} & n_{23} & n_{24} \\ n_{31} & n_{32} & n_{33} & n_{34} \end{bmatrix}$$

A **diagonal matrix** is a square matrix that has a zero for every element in the matrix except the elements on the main diagonal. All the elements on the main diagonal must be nonzero numbers.

$$\begin{bmatrix} n_{11} & 0 & 0 & 0 \\ 0 & n_{22} & 0 & 0 \\ 0 & 0 & n_{33} & 0 \\ 0 & 0 & 0 & n_{44} \end{bmatrix}$$

If every element on the main diagonal of a diagonal matrix is equal to one, the matrix is called an **identity matrix**. The identity matrix is often represented by the letter I.

$$I = \begin{bmatrix} 1 & 0 & 0 & 0 \\ 0 & 1 & 0 & 0 \\ 0 & 0 & 1 & 0 \\ 0 & 0 & 0 & 1 \end{bmatrix}$$

A **zero matrix** is a matrix that has zero as the value for every element in the matrix.

$$\begin{bmatrix} 0 & 0 & 0 & 0 \\ 0 & 0 & 0 & 0 \\ 0 & 0 & 0 & 0 \\ 0 & 0 & 0 & 0 \end{bmatrix}$$

The zero matrix is the *identity for matrix addition*. Do not confuse the zero matrix with the identity matrix.

The **negative of a matrix** is also known as the additive inverse of a matrix. If matrix N is the given matrix, then matrix $-N$ is its negative. This means that every element n_{ab} is equal to $-n_{ab}$ in the negative. To find the negative of a given matrix, change the sign of every element in the matrix and keep all elements in their original corresponding positions in the matrix.

If two matrices have the same order and all corresponding elements in the two matrices are the same, then the two matrices are **equal matrices**.

A matrix N may be **transposed** to matrix N^T by changing all rows into columns and changing all columns into rows. The easiest way to accomplish this is to swap the positions of the row and column notations for each element. For example, suppose the element in the second row of the third column of matrix N is $n_{23} = 6$. In the transposed matrix N^T, the transposed element would be $n_{32} = 6$, and it would be placed in the third row of the second column.

$$N = \begin{bmatrix} 1 & 2 & 3 \\ 4 & 5 & 6 \end{bmatrix}; \ N^T = \begin{bmatrix} 1 & 4 \\ 2 & 5 \\ 3 & 6 \end{bmatrix}$$

To quickly transpose a matrix by hand, begin with the first column and rewrite a new matrix with those same elements in the same order in the first row. Write the elements from the second column of the original matrix in the second row of the transposed matrix. Continue this process until all columns have been completed. If the original matrix is identical to the transposed matrix, the matrices are symmetric.

The **determinant** of a matrix is a scalar value that is calculated by taking into account all the elements of a square matrix. A determinant only exists for square matrices. Finding the determinant of a 2×2 matrix is as simple as remembering a simple equation. For a 2×2 matrix $M = \begin{bmatrix} m_{11} & m_{12} \\ m_{21} & m_{22} \end{bmatrix}$, the determinant is obtained by the equation $|M| = m_{11}m_{22} - m_{12}m_{21}$. Anything larger than 2×2 requires multiple steps. Take matrix $N = \begin{bmatrix} a & b & c \\ d & e & f \\ g & h & j \end{bmatrix}$. The determinant of N is calculated as $|N| = a \begin{vmatrix} e & f \\ h & j \end{vmatrix} - b \begin{vmatrix} d & f \\ g & j \end{vmatrix} + c \begin{vmatrix} d & e \\ g & h \end{vmatrix}$ or $|N| = a(ej - fh) - b(dj - fg) + c(dh - eg)$.

There is a shortcut for 3×3 matrices: add the products of each unique set of elements diagonally left-to-right and subtract the products of each unique set of elements diagonally right-to-left. In matrix N, the left-to-right diagonal elements are (a, e, j), (b, f, g), and (c, d, h). The right-to-left diagonal elements are (a, f, h), (b, d, j), and (c, e, g). $\det(N) = aej + bfg + cdh - afh - bdj - ceg$.

Calculating the determinants of matrices larger than 3×3 is rarely, if ever, done by hand.

The **inverse** of a matrix M is the matrix that, when multiplied by matrix M, yields a product that is the identity matrix. Multiplication of matrices will be explained in greater detail shortly. Not all matrices have inverses. Only a square matrix whose determinant is not zero has an inverse. If a matrix has an inverse, that inverse is unique to that matrix. For any matrix M that has an inverse, the inverse is represented by the symbol M^{-1}. To calculate the inverse of a 2×2 square matrix, use the following pattern:

$$M = \begin{bmatrix} m_{11} & m_{12} \\ m_{21} & m_{22} \end{bmatrix}; \ M^{-1} = \begin{bmatrix} \dfrac{m_{22}}{|M|} & \dfrac{-m_{12}}{|M|} \\ \dfrac{-m_{21}}{|M|} & \dfrac{m_{11}}{|M|} \end{bmatrix}$$

Another way to find the inverse of a matrix by hand is use an augmented matrix and elementary row operations. An **augmented matrix** is is formed by appending the entries from one matrix onto the end of another. For example, given a 2×2 invertible matrix $N = \begin{bmatrix} a & b \\ c & d \end{bmatrix}$, you can find the inverse N^{-1} by creating an augmented matrix by appending a 2×2 identity matrix: $\left[\begin{array}{cc|cc} a & b & 1 & 0 \\ c & d & 0 & 1 \end{array}\right]$. To find the inverse of the original 2×2 matrix, perform elementary row operations to convert the original matrix on the left to an identity matrix: $\left[\begin{array}{cc|cc} 1 & 0 & e & f \\ 0 & 1 & g & h \end{array}\right]$. **Elementary row operations** include multiplying a row by a non-zero scalar, adding scalar multiples of two rows, or some combination of these. For instance, the first step might be to multiply the second row by $\frac{b}{d}$ and then subtract it from the first row to make its second column a zero. The end result is that the 2×2 section on the right will become the inverse of the original matrix: $N^{-1} = \begin{bmatrix} e & f \\ g & h \end{bmatrix}$.

Calculating the inverse of any matrix larger than 2×2 is cumbersome and using a graphing calculator is recommended.

Basic Operations with Matrices
There are two categories of basic operations with regard to matrices: operations between a matrix and a scalar, and operations between two matrices.

Scalar Operations
A scalar being added to a matrix is treated as though it were being added to each element of the matrix:
$$M + 4 = \begin{bmatrix} m_{11} + 4 & m_{12} + 4 \\ m_{21} + 4 & m_{22} + 4 \end{bmatrix}$$
The same is true for the other three operations. Subtraction:
$$M - 4 = \begin{bmatrix} m_{11} - 4 & m_{12} - 4 \\ m_{21} - 4 & m_{22} - 4 \end{bmatrix}$$
Multiplication:
$$M \times 4 = \begin{bmatrix} m_{11} \times 4 & m_{12} \times 4 \\ m_{21} \times 4 & m_{22} \times 4 \end{bmatrix}$$
Division:
$$M \div 4 = \begin{bmatrix} m_{11} \div 4 & m_{12} \div 4 \\ m_{21} \div 4 & m_{22} \div 4 \end{bmatrix}$$

Matrix Addition and Subtraction
All four of the basic operations can be used with operations between matrices (although division is usually discarded in favor of multiplication by the inverse), but there are restrictions on the

situations in which they can be used. Matrices that meet all the qualifications for a given operation are called **conformable matrices**. However, conformability is specific to the operation; two matrices that are conformable for addition are not necessarily conformable for multiplication.

For two matrices to be conformable for addition or subtraction, they must be of the same dimension; otherwise the operation is not defined. If matrix M is a 3×2 matrix and matrix N is a 2×3 matrix, the operations $M + N$ and $M - N$ are meaningless. If matrices M and N are the same size, the operation is as simple as adding or subtracting all of the corresponding elements:

$$\begin{bmatrix} m_{11} & m_{12} \\ m_{21} & m_{22} \end{bmatrix} + \begin{bmatrix} n_{11} & n_{12} \\ n_{21} & n_{22} \end{bmatrix} = \begin{bmatrix} m_{11} + n_{11} & m_{12} + n_{12} \\ m_{21} + n_{21} & m_{22} + n_{22} \end{bmatrix}$$

$$\begin{bmatrix} m_{11} & m_{12} \\ m_{21} & m_{22} \end{bmatrix} - \begin{bmatrix} n_{11} & n_{12} \\ n_{21} & n_{22} \end{bmatrix} = \begin{bmatrix} m_{11} - n_{11} & m_{12} - n_{12} \\ m_{21} - n_{21} & m_{22} - n_{22} \end{bmatrix}$$

The result of addition or subraction is a matrix of the same dimension as the two original matrices involved in the operation.

Multiplication
The first thing it is necessary to understand about matrix multiplication is that it is not commutative. In scalar multiplication, the operation is commutative, meaning that $a \times b = b \times a$. For matrix multiplication, this is not the case: $A \times B \neq B \times A$. The terminology must be specific when describing matrix multiplication. The operation $A \times B$ can be described as A multiplied (or **postmultiplied**) by B, or B **premultiplied** by A.

For two matrices to be conformable for multiplication, they need not be of the same dimension, but specific dimensions must correspond. Taking the example of two matrices M and N to be multiplied $M \times N$, matrix M must have the same number of columns as matrix N has rows. Put another way, if matrix M has the dimensions $a \times b$ and matrix N has the dimensions $c \times d$, b must equal c if the two matrices are to be conformable for this multiplication. The matrix that results from the multiplication will have the dimensions $a \times d$. If a and d are both equal to 1, the product is simply a scalar. Square matrices of the same dimensions are always conformable for multiplication, and their product is always a matrix of the same size.

The simplest type of matrix multiplication is a 1×2 matrix (a row vector) times a 2×1 matrix (a column vector). These will multiply in the following way:

$$[m_{11} \quad m_{12}] \times \begin{bmatrix} n_{11} \\ n_{21} \end{bmatrix} = m_{11}n_{11} + m_{12}n_{21}$$

The two matrices are conformable for multiplication because matrix M has the same number of columns as matrix N has rows. Because the other dimensions are both 1, the result is a scalar. Expanding our matrices to 1×3 and 3×1, the process is the same:

$$[m_{11} \quad m_{12} \quad m_{13}] \times \begin{bmatrix} n_{11} \\ n_{21} \\ n_{31} \end{bmatrix} = m_{11}n_{11} + m_{12}n_{21} + m_{13}n_{31}$$

Once again, the result is a scalar. This type of basic matrix multiplication is the building block for the multiplication of larger matrices.

To multiply larger matrices, treat each **row from the first matrix** and each **column from the second matrix** as individual vectors and follow the pattern for multiplying vectors. The scalar value found from multiplying the first row vector by the first column vector is placed in the first row, first column of the new matrix. The scalar value found from multiplying the second row vector by the first column vector is placed in the second row, first column of the new matrix. Continue this pattern until each row of the first matrix has been multiplied by each column of the second vector. Below is an example of the multiplication of a 3×2 matrix and a 2×3 matrix.

$$\begin{bmatrix} m_{11} & m_{12} \\ m_{21} & m_{22} \\ m_{31} & m_{32} \end{bmatrix} \times \begin{bmatrix} n_{11} & n_{12} & n_{13} \\ n_{21} & n_{22} & n_{23} \end{bmatrix} = \begin{bmatrix} m_{11}n_{11} + m_{12}n_{21} & m_{11}n_{12} + m_{12}n_{22} & m_{11}n_{13} + m_{12}n_{23} \\ m_{21}n_{11} + m_{22}n_{21} & m_{21}n_{12} + m_{22}n_{22} & m_{21}n_{13} + m_{22}n_{23} \\ m_{31}n_{11} + m_{32}n_{21} & m_{31}n_{12} + m_{32}n_{22} & m_{31}n_{13} + m_{32}n_{23} \end{bmatrix}$$

The result is a 3×3 matrix. If the operation were done in reverse $(N \times M)$, the result would be a 2×2 matrix.

$$\begin{bmatrix} n_{11} & n_{12} & n_{13} \\ n_{21} & n_{22} & n_{23} \end{bmatrix} \times \begin{bmatrix} m_{11} & m_{12} \\ m_{21} & m_{22} \\ m_{31} & m_{32} \end{bmatrix} = \begin{bmatrix} m_{11}n_{11} + m_{21}n_{12} + m_{31}n_{13} & m_{12}n_{11} + m_{22}n_{12} + m_{32}n_{13} \\ m_{11}n_{21} + m_{21}n_{22} + m_{31}n_{23} & m_{12}n_{21} + m_{22}n_{22} + m_{32}n_{23} \end{bmatrix}$$

Solving systems of equations

Matrices can be used to represent the coefficients of a system of linear equations and can be very useful in solving those systems. Take for instance three equations with three variables:

$$a_1 x + b_1 y + c_1 z = d_1$$
$$a_2 x + b_2 y + c_2 z = d_2$$
$$a_3 x + b_3 y + c_3 z = d_3$$

where all a, b, c, and d are known constants. To solve this system, define three matrices:

$$A = \begin{bmatrix} a_1 & b_1 & c_1 \\ a_2 & b_2 & c_2 \\ a_3 & b_3 & c_3 \end{bmatrix}; \ D = \begin{bmatrix} d_1 \\ d_2 \\ d_3 \end{bmatrix}; \ X = \begin{bmatrix} x \\ y \\ z \end{bmatrix}$$

The three equations in our system can be fully represented by a single matrix equation:

$$AX = D$$

We know that the identity matrix times X is equal to X, and we know that any matrix multiplied by its inverse is equal to the identity matrix.

$$A^{-1}AX = IX = X; \text{thus } X = A^{-1}D$$

Our goal then is to find the inverse of A, or A^{-1}. Once we have that, we can premultiply matrix D by A^{-1} (postmultiplying here is an undefined operation) to find matrix X.

Systems of equations can also be solved using the transformation of an augmented matrix in a process similar to that for finding a matrix inverse. Begin by arranging each equation of the system in the following format:

$$a_1 x + b_1 y + c_1 z = d_1$$
$$a_2 x + b_2 y + c_2 z = d_2$$

$$a_3x + b_3y + c_3z = d_3$$

Define matrices A and D and combine them into augmented matrix A_a:

$$A = \begin{bmatrix} a_1 & b_1 & c_1 \\ a_2 & b_2 & c_2 \\ a_3 & b_3 & c_3 \end{bmatrix}; \ D = \begin{bmatrix} d_1 \\ d_2 \\ d_3 \end{bmatrix}; \ A_a = \begin{bmatrix} a_1 & b_1 & c_1 & d_1 \\ a_2 & b_2 & c_2 & d_2 \\ a_3 & b_3 & c_3 & d_3 \end{bmatrix}$$

To solve the augmented matrix and the system of equations, use elementary row operations to form an identity matrix in the first 3×3 section. When this is complete, the values in the last column are the solutions to the system of equations:

$$\begin{bmatrix} 1 & 0 & 0 & x \\ 0 & 1 & 0 & y \\ 0 & 0 & 1 & z \end{bmatrix}$$

If an identity matrix is not possible, the system of equations has no unique solution. Sometimes only a partial solution will be possible. The following are partial solutions you may find:

$$\begin{bmatrix} 1 & 0 & k_1 & x_0 \\ 0 & 1 & k_2 & y_0 \\ 0 & 0 & 0 & 0 \end{bmatrix}$$ gives the non-unique solution $x = x_0 - k_1z; \ y = y_0 - k_2z$

$$\begin{bmatrix} 1 & j_1 & k_1 & x_0 \\ 0 & 0 & 0 & 0 \\ 0 & 0 & 0 & 0 \end{bmatrix}$$ gives the non-unique solution $x = x_0 - j_1y - k_1z$

This process can be used to solve systems of equations with any number of variables, but three is the upper limit for practical purposes. Anything more ought to be done with a graphing calculator.

Geometric transformations

The four geometric transformations are translations, reflections, rotations, and dilations. When geometric transformations are expressed as matrices, the process of performing the transformations is simplified. For calculations of the geometric transformations of a planar figure, make a $2 \times n$ matrix, where n is the number of vertices in the planar figure. Each column represents the rectangular coordinates of one vertex of the figure, with the top row containing the values of the x-coordinates and the bottom row containing the values of the y-coordinates. For example, given a planar triangular figure with coordinates (x_1, y_1), (x_2, y_2), and (x_3, y_3), the corresponding matrix is $\begin{bmatrix} x_1 & x_2 & x_3 \\ y_1 & y_2 & y_3 \end{bmatrix}$. You can then perform the necessary transformations on this matrix to determine the coordinates of the resulting figure.

Translation

A translation moves a figure along the x-axis, the y-axis, or both axes without changing the size or shape of the figure. To calculate the new coordinates of a planar figure following a translation, set up a matrix of the coordinates and a matrix of the translation values and add the two matrices.

$$\begin{bmatrix} h & h & h \\ v & v & v \end{bmatrix} + \begin{bmatrix} x_1 & x_2 & x_3 \\ y_1 & y_2 & y_3 \end{bmatrix} = \begin{bmatrix} h + x_1 & h + x_2 & h + x_3 \\ v + y_1 & v + y_2 & v + y_3 \end{bmatrix}$$

where h is the number of units the figure is moved along the x-axis (horizontally) and v is the number of units the figure is moved along the y-axis (vertically).

Reflection

To find the reflection of a planar figure over the x-axis, set up a matrix of the coordinates of the vertices and pre-multiply the matrix by the 2×2 matrix $\begin{bmatrix} 1 & 0 \\ 0 & -1 \end{bmatrix}$ so that $\begin{bmatrix} 1 & 0 \\ 0 & -1 \end{bmatrix} \begin{bmatrix} x_1 & x_2 & x_3 \\ y_1 & y_2 & y_3 \end{bmatrix} =$ $\begin{bmatrix} x_1 & x_2 & x_3 \\ -y_1 & -y_2 & -y_3 \end{bmatrix}$. To find the reflection of a planar figure over the y-axis, set up a matrix of the coordinates of the vertices and pre-multiply the matrix by the 2×2 matrix $\begin{bmatrix} -1 & 0 \\ 0 & 1 \end{bmatrix}$ so that $\begin{bmatrix} -1 & 0 \\ 0 & 1 \end{bmatrix} \begin{bmatrix} x_1 & x_2 & x_3 \\ y_1 & y_2 & y_3 \end{bmatrix} = \begin{bmatrix} -x_1 & -x_2 & -x_3 \\ y_1 & y_2 & y_3 \end{bmatrix}$. To find the reflection of a planar figure over the line $y = x$, set up a matrix of the coordinates of the vertices and pre-multiply the matrix by the 2×2 matrix $\begin{bmatrix} 0 & 1 \\ 1 & 0 \end{bmatrix}$ so that $\begin{bmatrix} 0 & 1 \\ 1 & 0 \end{bmatrix} \begin{bmatrix} x_1 & x_2 & x_3 \\ y_1 & y_2 & y_3 \end{bmatrix} = \begin{bmatrix} y_1 & y_2 & y_3 \\ x_1 & x_2 & x_3 \end{bmatrix}$. Remember that the order of multiplication is important when multiplying matrices. The commutative property does not apply.

Rotation

To find the coordinates of the figure formed by rotating a planar figure about the origin θ degrees in a counterclockwise direction, set up a matrix of the coordinates of the vertices and pre-multiply the matrix by the 2×2 matrix $\begin{bmatrix} \cos \theta & \sin \theta \\ -\sin \theta & \cos \theta \end{bmatrix}$. For example, if you want to rotate a figure $90°$ clockwise around the origin, you would have to convert the degree measure to $270°$ counterclockwise and solve the 2×2 matrix you have set as the pre-multiplier: $\begin{bmatrix} \cos 270° & \sin 270° \\ -\sin 270° & \cos 270° \end{bmatrix} = \begin{bmatrix} 0 & -1 \\ 1 & 0 \end{bmatrix}$. Use this as the pre-multiplier for the matrix $\begin{bmatrix} x_1 & x_2 & x_3 \\ y_1 & y_2 & y_3 \end{bmatrix}$ and solve to find the new coordinates.

Dilation

To find the dilation of a planar figure by a scale factor of k, set up a matrix of the coordinates of the vertices of the planar figure and pre-multiply the matrix by the 2×2 matrix $\begin{bmatrix} k & 0 \\ 0 & k \end{bmatrix}$ so that $\begin{bmatrix} k & 0 \\ 0 & k \end{bmatrix} \begin{bmatrix} x_1 & x_2 & x_3 \\ y_1 & y_2 & y_3 \end{bmatrix} = \begin{bmatrix} kx_1 & kx_2 & kx_3 \\ ky_1 & ky_2 & ky_3 \end{bmatrix}$. This is effectively the same as multiplying the matrix by the scalar k, but the matrix equation would still be necessary if the figure were being dilated by different factors in vertical and horizontal directions. The scale factor k will be positive if the figure is being enlarged, and negative if the figure is being shrunk. Again, remember that when multiplying matrices, the order of the matrices is important. The commutative property does not apply, and the matrix with the coordinates of the figure must be the second matrix.

Discrete Math

Sequences

A sequence is a set of numbers that continues on in a define pattern. The function that defines a sequence has a domain composed of the set of positive integers. Each member of the sequence is an element, or individual term. Each element is identified by the notation a_n, where a is the term of the sequence, and n is the integer identifying which term in the sequence a is. There are two different ways to represent a sequence that contains the element a_n. The first is the simple notation $\{a_n\}$. The expanded notation of a sequence is $a_1, a_2, a_3, \ldots a_n, \ldots$. Notice that the expanded form does not end with the nth term. There is no indication that the nth term is the last term in the sequence, only that the nth term is an element of the sequence.

Some sequences will have a limit, or a value the sequence approaches or sometimes even reaches but never passes. A sequence that has a limit is known as a convergent sequence because all the values of the sequence seemingly converge at that point. Sequences that do not converge at a particular limit are divergent sequences. The easiest way to determine whether a sequence converges or diverges is to find the limit of the sequence. If the limit is a real number, the sequence is a convergent sequence. If the limit is infinity, the sequence is a divergent sequence. Remember the following rules for finding limits:

$\lim_{n \to \infty} k = k$ for all real numbers k

$\lim_{n \to \infty} \frac{1}{n} = 0$

$\lim_{n \to \infty} n = \infty$

$\lim_{n \to \infty} \frac{k}{n^p} = 0$ for all real numbers k and positive rational numbers p.

The limit of the sums of two sequences is equal to the sum of the limits of the two sequences:
$\lim_{n \to \infty}(a_n + b_n) = \lim_{n \to \infty} a_n + \lim_{n \to \infty} b_n$.
The limit of the difference between two sequences is equal to the difference between the limits of the two sequences:
$\lim_{n \to \infty}(a_n - b_n) = \lim_{n \to \infty} a_n - \lim_{n \to \infty} b_n$.
The limit of the product of two sequences is equal to the product of the limits of the two sequences:
$\lim_{n \to \infty}(a_n \cdot b_n) = \lim_{n \to \infty} a_n \cdot \lim_{n \to \infty} b_n$.
The limit of the quotient of two sequences is equal to the quotient of the limits of the two sequences, with some exceptions: $\lim_{n \to \infty} \left(\frac{a_n}{b_n}\right) = \frac{\lim_{n \to \infty} a_n}{\lim_{n \to \infty} b_n}$. In the quotient formula, it is important to consider that $b_n \neq 0$ and $\lim_{n \to \infty} b_n \neq 0$.
The limit of a sequence multiplied by a scalar is equal to the scalar multiplied by the limit of the sequence: $\lim_{n \to \infty} k a_n = k \lim_{n \to \infty} a_n$, where k is any real number.

A **monotonic sequence** is a sequence that is either nonincreasing or nondecreasing. The term *nonincreasing* is used to describe a sequence whose terms either get progressively smaller in value or remain the same. The term *nondecreasing* is used to describe a sequence whose terms either get progressively larger in value or remain the same. A nonincreasing sequence is bounded above. This means that all elements of the sequence must be less than a given real number. A nondecreasing sequence is bounded below. This means that all elements of the sequence must be greater than a given real number.

When one element of a sequence is defined in terms of a previous element or elements of the sequence, the sequence is a **recursive sequence**. For example, given the recursive definition $a_1 = 0$; $a_2 = 1$; $a_n = a_{n-1} + a_{n-2}$ for all $n \geq 2$, you get the sequence 0, 1, 1, 2, 3, 5, 8, …. This particular sequence is known as the Fibonacci sequence, and is defined as the numbers zero and one, and a continuing sequence of numbers, with each number in the sequence equal to the sum of the two previous numbers. It is important to note that the Fibonacci sequence can also be defined as the first two terms being equal to one, with the remaining terms equal to the sum of the previous two terms. Both definitions are considered correct in mathematics. Make sure you know which definition you are working with when dealing with Fibonacci numbers.

Sometimes one term of a sequence with a recursive definition can be found without knowing the previous terms of the sequence. This case is known as a closed-form expression for a recursive definition. In this case, an alternate formula will apply to the sequence to generate the same sequence of numbers. However, not all sequences based on recursive definitions will have a closed-form expression. Some sequences will require the use of the recursive definition. For example, the Fibonacci sequence has a closed-form expression given by the formula $a_n = \frac{\phi^n - \left(\frac{-1}{\phi}\right)^n}{\sqrt{5}}$, where φ is the golden ratio, which is equal to $\frac{1+\sqrt{5}}{2}$. In this case, $a_0 = 0$ and $a_1 = 1$, so you know which definition of the Fibonacci sequence you have.

An **arithmetic sequence**, or arithmetic progression, is a special kind of sequence in which each term has a specific quantity, called the common difference, that is added to the previous term. The common difference may be positive or negative. The general form of an arithmetic sequence containing n terms is $a_1, a_1 + d, a_1 + 2d, \ldots, a_1 + (n-1)d$, where d is the common difference. The formula for the general term of an arithmetic sequence is $a_n = a_1 + (n-1)d$, where a_n is the term you are looking for and d is the common difference. To find the sum of the first n terms of an arithmetic sequence, use the formula $s_n = \frac{n}{2}(a_1 + a_n)$.

A **geometric sequence**, or geometric progression, is a special kind of sequence in which each term has a specific quantity, called the common ratio, multiplied by the previous term. The common ratio may be positive or negative. The general form of a geometric sequence containing n terms is $a_1, a_1 r, a_1 r^2, \ldots, a_1 r^{n-1}$, where r is the common ratio. The formula for the general term of a geometric sequence is $a_n = a_1 r^{n-1}$, where a_n is the term you are looking for and r is the common ratio. To find the sum of the first n terms of a geometric sequence, use the formula $s_n = \frac{a_1(1-r^n)}{1-r}$.

Any function with the set of all natural numbers as the domain is also called a sequence. An element of a sequence is denoted by the symbol a_n, which represents the nth element of sequence a. Sequences may be arithmetic or geometric, and may be defined by a recursive definition, closed-form expression or both. Arithmetic and geometric sequences both have recursive definitions based on the first term of the sequence, as well as both having formulas to find the sum of the first n terms in the sequence, assuming you know what the first term is. The sum of all the terms in a sequence is called a **series**.

Series

An infinite series, also referred to as just a series, is a series of partial sums of a defined sequence. Each infinite sequence represents an infinite series according to the equation $\sum_{n=1}^{\infty} a_n = a_1 + a_2 + a_3 + \cdots + a_n + \cdots$. This notation can be shortened to $\sum_{n=1}^{\infty} a_n$ or $\sum a_n$. Every series is a sequence of partial sums, where the first partial sum is equal to the first element of the series, the second partial sum is equal to the sum of the first two elements of the series, and the nth partial sum is equal to the sum of the first n elements of the series.

Every infinite sequence of partial sums (infinite series) either converges or diverges. Like the test for convergence in a sequence, finding the limit of the sequence of partial sums will indicate whether it is a converging series or a diverging series. If there exists a real number S such that $\lim_{n \to \infty} S_n = S$, where S_n is the sequence of partial sums, then the series converges. If the limit equals infinity, then the series diverges. If $\lim_{n \to \infty} S_n = S$ and S is a real number, then S is also the convergence value of the series.

To find the sum as n approaches infinity for the sum of two convergent series, find the sum as n approaches infinity for each individual series and add the results.

$$\sum_{n=1}^{\infty} (a_n + b_n) = \sum_{n=1}^{\infty} a_n + \sum_{n=1}^{\infty} b_n$$

To find the sum as n approaches infinity for the difference between two convergent series, find the sum as n approaches infinity for each individual series and subtract the results.

$$\sum_{n=1}^{\infty} (a_n - b_n) = \sum_{n=1}^{\infty} a_n - \sum_{n=1}^{\infty} b_n$$

To find the sum as n approaches infinity for the product of a scalar and a convergent series, find the sum as n approaches infinity for the series and multiply the result by the scalar.

$$\sum_{n=1}^{\infty} k a_n = k \sum_{n=1}^{\infty} a_n$$

A **geometric series** is an infinite series in which each term is multiplied by a constant real number r, called the ratio. This is represented by the equation

$$\sum_{n=1}^{\infty} a r^{n-1} = a_1 + a_2 r + a_3 r^2 + \cdots + a_n r^{n-1} + \cdots$$

If the absolute value of r is greater than or equal to one, then the geometric series is a diverging series. If the absolute value of r is less than one but greater than zero, the geometric series is a converging series. To find the sum of a converging geometric series, use the formula

$$\sum_{n=1}^{\infty} a r^{n-1} = \frac{a}{1-r}, \text{ where } 0 < |r| < 1$$

The **nth term test for divergence** involves taking the limit of the nth term of a sequence and determining whether or not the limit is equal to zero. If the limit of the nth term is not equal to zero, then the series is a diverging series. This test only works to prove divergence, however. If the nth term is equal to zero, the test is inconclusive.

Cartesian products/relations

A Cartesian product is the product of two sets of data, X and Y, such that all elements x are a member of set X, and all elements y are a member of set Y. The product of the two sets, $X \times Y$ is the set of all ordered pairs (x, y). For example, given a standard deck of 52 playing cards, there are four possible suits (hearts, diamonds, clubs, and spades) and thirteen possible card values (the numbers 2 through 10, ace, jack, queen, and king). If the card suits are set X and the card values are set Y, then there are $4 \times 13 = 52$ possible different (x, y) combinations, as seen in the 52 cards of a standard deck.

A binary relation, also referred to as a relation, dyadic relation, or 2-place relation, is a subset of a Cartesian product. It shows the relation between one set of objects and a second set of object, or between one set of objects and itself. The prefix *bi*- means *two*, so there are always two sets involved – either two different sets, or the same set used twice. The ordered pairs of the Cartesian product are used to indicate a binary relation. Relations are possible for situations involving more than two sets, but those are not called binary relations.

The five types of relations are reflexive, symmetric, transitive, antisymmetric, and equivalence. A reflexive relation has $x \Re x$ (x related to x) for all values of x in the set. A symmetric relation has $x \Re y \Rightarrow y \Re x$ for all values of x and y in the set. A transitive relation has $(x \Re y$ and $y \Re z) \Rightarrow x \Re z$ for all values of x, y, and z in the set. An antisymmetric relation has $(x \Re y$ and $y \Re x) \Rightarrow x = y$ for all values of x and y in the set. A relation that is reflexive, symmetric, and transitive is called an equivalence relation.

Vertex-edge graphs

A vertex-edge graph is a set of items or objects connected by pathways or links. Below is a picture of a very basic vertex-edge graph.

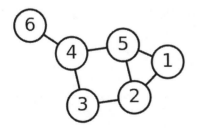

Vertex-edge graphs are useful for solving problems involving schedules, relationships, networks, or paths among a set number of objects. The number of objects may be large, but it will never be infinite. The vertices or points on the graph represent the objects and are referred to as *nodes*. The nodes are joined by line segments called *edges* or links that show the specific paths that connect the various elements represented by the nodes. The number of nodes does not have to equal the number of edges. There may be more or less, depending on the number of allowable paths.

An endpoint on a vertex-edge graph is a vertex on exactly one edge. In the case of a vertex that is an endpoint, the edge that the vertex is on is incident with the vertex. Two edges are considered to be adjacent if they share a vertex. Two vertices are considered to be adjacent if they share an edge.

In a vertex-edge graph, a loop is an edge that has the same vertex as both endpoints. To calculate the degree of a vertex in a vertex-edge graph, count the number of edges that are incident with the vertex, counting loops twice since they meet the vertex at both ends. The degree sum formula states that the sum of the degrees of all vertices on a vertex-edge graph is always equal to twice the number of edges on the graph. Thus, the sum of the degrees will never be odd, even if there are an odd number of vertices.

In a vertex-edge graph, a path is a given sequence of vertices that follows one or more edges to get from vertex to vertex. There is no jumping over spaces to get from one vertex to the next, although doubling back over an edge already traveled is allowed. A simple path is a path that does not repeat an edge in traveling from beginning to end. Think of the vertex-edge graph as a map, with the vertices as cities on the map, and the edges as roads between the cities. To get from one city to another, you must drive on the roads. A simple path allows you to complete your trip without driving on the same road twice.

In a vertex-edge graph, a circuit is a path that has the same starting and stopping point. Picturing the vertex-edge graph as a map with cities and roads, a circuit is like leaving home on vacation and then returning home after you have visited your intended destinations. You may go in one direction and then turn around, or you may go in a circle. A simple circuit on the graph completes the circuit without repeating an edge. This is like going on vacation without driving on the same road twice.

On a vertex-edge graph, any path that uses each edge exactly one time is called an Euler path. One simple way to rule out the possibility of an Euler path is to calculate the degree of each vertex. If more than two vertices have an odd degree, an Euler path is impossible. A path that uses each vertex exactly one time is called a Hamiltonian path.
If every pair of vertices is joined by an edge, the vertex-edge graph is said to be connected. If the vertex-edge graph has no simple circuits in it, then the graph is said to be a tree.

For additional review help, please check out our COMPASS math review tutorials, which can be found on the Mometrix Academy:

http://www.mometrix.com/academy/compass-mathematics/

Reading Test

Understanding Literature

Reading literature is a different experience than reading non-fiction works. Our imagination is more active as we review what we have read, imagine ourselves as characters in the novel, and try to guess what will happen next. Suspense, surprise, fantasy, fear, anxiety, compassion, and a host of other emotions and feelings may be stirred by a provocative novel.

Reading longer works of fiction is a cumulative process. Some elements of a novel have a great impact, while others may go virtually unnoticed. Therefore, as novels are read with a critical eye to language, it is helpful to perceive and identify larger patterns and movements in the work as a whole. This will benefit the reader by placing characters and events in perspective, and will enrich the reading experience greatly. Novels should be savored rather than gulped. Careful reading and thoughtful analysis of the major themes of the novel are essential to a clear understanding of the work.

One of the most important skills in reading comprehension is the identification of **topics** and **main ideas.** There is a subtle difference between these two features. The topic is the subject of a text, or what the text is about. The main idea, on the other hand, is the most important point being made by the author. The topic is usually expressed in a few words at the most, while the main idea often needs a full sentence to be completely defined. As an example, a short passage might have the topic of penguins and the main idea *Penguins are different from other birds in many ways*. In most nonfiction writing, the topic and the main idea will be stated directly, often in a sentence at the very beginning or end of the text. When being tested on an understanding of the author's topic, the reader can quickly *skim* the passage for the general idea, stopping to read only the first sentence of each paragraph. A paragraph's first sentence is often (but not always) the main topic sentence, and it gives you a summary of the content of the paragraph. However, there are cases in which the reader must figure out an unstated topic or main idea. In these instances, the student must read every sentence of the text, and try to come up with an overarching idea that is supported by each of those sentences.

While the main idea is the overall premise of a story, **supporting details** provide evidence and backing for the main point. In order to show that a main idea is correct, or valid, the author needs to add details that prove their point. All texts contain details, but they are only classified as supporting details when they serve to reinforce some larger point. Supporting details are most commonly found in informative and persuasive texts. In some cases, they will be clearly indicated with words like *for example* or *for instance*, or they will be enumerated with words like *first*, *second*, and *last*. However, they may not be indicated with special words. As a reader, it is important to consider whether the author's supporting details really back up his or her main point. Supporting details can be factual and correct but still not relevant to the author's point. Conversely, supporting details can seem pertinent but be ineffective because they are based on opinion or assertions that cannot be proven.

An example of a main idea is: "Giraffes live in the Serengeti of Africa." A supporting detail about giraffes could be: "A giraffe uses its long neck to reach twigs and leaves on trees." The main idea gives the general idea that the text is about giraffes. The supporting detail gives a specific fact about how the giraffes eat.

As opposed to a main idea, themes are seldom expressed directly in a text, so they can be difficult to identify. A **theme** is an issue, an idea, or a question raised by the text. For instance, a theme of William Shakespeare's *Hamlet* is indecision, as the title character explores his own psyche and the results of his failure to make bold choices. A great work of literature may have many themes, and the reader is justified in identifying any for which he or she can find support. One common characteristic of themes is that they raise more questions than they answer. In a good piece of fiction, the author is not always trying to convince the reader, but is instead trying to elevate the reader's perspective and encourage him to consider the themes more deeply. When reading, one can identify themes by constantly asking what general issues the text is addressing. A good way to evaluate an author's approach to a theme is to begin reading with a question in mind (for example, how does this text approach the theme of love?) and then look for evidence in the text that addresses that question.

> ➢ **Review Video: Theme**
> *Visit **mometrix.com/academy** and enter **Code: 732074***

Purposes for Writing

In order to be an effective reader, one must pay attention to the author's **position** and purpose. Even those texts that seem objective and impartial, like textbooks, have some sort of position and bias. Readers need to take these positions into account when considering the author's message. When an author uses emotional language or clearly favors one side of an argument, his position is clear. However, the author's position may be evident not only in what he writes, but in what he doesn't write. For this reason, it is sometimes necessary to review some other texts on the same topic in order to develop a view of the author's position. If this is not possible, then it may be useful to acquire a little background personal information about the author. When the only source of information is the text, however, the reader should look for language and argumentation that seems to indicate a particular stance on the subject.

Identifying the **purpose** of an author is usually easier than identifying her position. In most cases, the author has no interest in hiding his or her purpose. A text that is meant to entertain, for instance, should be obviously written to please the reader. Most narratives, or stories, are written to entertain, though they may also inform or persuade. Informative texts are easy to identify as well. The most difficult purpose of a text to identify is persuasion, because the author has an interest in making this purpose hard to detect. When a person knows that the author is trying to convince him, he is automatically more wary and skeptical of the argument. For this reason persuasive texts often try to establish an entertaining tone, hoping to amuse the reader into agreement, or an informative tone, hoping to create an appearance of authority and objectivity.

An author's purpose is often evident in the organization of the text. For instance, if the text has headings and subheadings, if key terms are in bold, and if the author makes his main idea clear from the beginning, then the likely purpose of the text is to inform. If the author begins by making a claim and then makes various arguments to support that claim, the purpose is probably to persuade. If the author is telling a story, or is more interested in holding the attention of the reader than in making a particular point or delivering information, then his purpose is most likely to entertain. As a reader, it is best to judge an author on how well he accomplishes his purpose. In other words, it is not entirely fair to complain that a textbook is boring: if the text is clear and easy to understand, then the author has done his job. Similarly, a storyteller should not be judged too harshly for getting some facts wrong, so long as he is able to give pleasure to the reader.

The author's purpose for writing will affect his writing style and the response of the reader. In a **persuasive essay**, the author is attempting to change the reader's mind or convince him of something he did not believe previously. There are several identifying characteristics of persuasive writing. One is opinion presented as fact. When an author attempts to persuade the reader, he often presents his or her opinions as if they were fact. A reader must be on guard for statements that sound factual but which cannot be subjected to research, observation, or experiment. Another characteristic of persuasive writing is emotional language. An author will often try to play on the reader's emotion by appealing to his sympathy or sense of morality. When an author uses colorful or evocative language with the intent of arousing the reader's passions, it is likely that he is attempting to persuade. Finally, in many cases a persuasive text will give an unfair explanation of opposing positions, if these positions are mentioned at all.

> ➢ **Review Video: Persuasive Essay**
> Visit **mometrix.com/academy** and enter **Code: 621428**

An **informative text** is written to educate and enlighten the reader. Informative texts are almost always nonfiction, and are rarely structured as a story. The intention of an informative text is to deliver information in the most comprehensible way possible, so the structure of the text is likely to be very clear. In an informative text, the thesis statement is often in the first sentence. The author may use some colorful language, but is likely to put more emphasis on clarity and precision. Informative essays do not typically appeal to the emotions. They often contain facts and figures, and rarely include the opinion of the author. Sometimes a persuasive essay can resemble an informative essay, especially if the author maintains an even tone and presents his or her views as if they were established fact.

The success or failure of an author's intent to **entertain** is determined by those who read the author's work. Entertaining texts may be either fiction or nonfiction, and they may describe real or imagined people, places, and events. Entertaining texts are often narratives, or stories. A text that is written to entertain is likely to contain colorful language that engages the imagination and the emotions. Such writing often features a great deal of figurative language, which typically enlivens its subject matter with images and analogies. Though an entertaining text is not usually written to persuade or inform, it may accomplish both of these tasks. An entertaining text may appeal to the reader's emotions and cause him or her to think differently about a particular subject. In any case, entertaining texts tend to showcase the personality of the author more so than do other types of writing.

When an author intends to **express feelings,** she may use colorful and evocative language. An author may write emotionally for any number of reasons. Sometimes, the author will do so because she is describing a personal situation of great pain or happiness. Sometimes an author is attempting to persuade the reader, and so will use emotion to stir up the passions. It can be easy to identify this kind of expression when the writer uses phrases like *I felt* and *I sense*. However, sometimes the author will simply describe feelings without introducing them. As a reader, it is important to recognize when an author is expressing emotion, and not to become overwhelmed by sympathy or passion. A reader should maintain some detachment so that he or she can still evaluate the strength of the author's argument or the quality of the writing.

In a sense, almost all writing is descriptive, insofar as it seeks to describe events, ideas, or people to the reader. Some texts, however, are primarily concerned with **description**. A descriptive text focuses on a particular subject, and attempts to depict it in a way that will be clear to the reader. Descriptive texts contain many adjectives and adverbs, words that give shades of meaning and create a more detailed mental picture for the reader. A descriptive text fails when it is unclear or vague to the reader. On the other hand, however, a descriptive text that compiles too much detail can be boring and overwhelming to the reader. A descriptive text will certainly be informative, and it may be persuasive and entertaining as well. Descriptive writing is a challenge for the author, but when it is done well, it can be fun to read.

Writing Devices

Authors will use different stylistic and writing devices to make their meaning more clearly understood. One of those devices is comparison and contrast. When an author describes the ways in which two things are alike, he or she is **comparing** them. When the author describes the ways in which two things are different, he or she is **contrasting** them. The "compare and contrast" essay is one of the most common forms in nonfiction. It is often signaled with certain words: a comparison may be indicated with such words as *both, same, like, too,* and *as well;* while a contrast may be indicated by words like *but, however, on the other hand, instead,* and *yet.* Of course, comparisons and contrasts may be implicit without using any such signaling language. A single sentence may both compare and contrast. Consider the sentence *Brian and Sheila love ice cream, but Brian prefers vanilla and Sheila prefers strawberry.* In one sentence, the author has described both a similarity (love of ice cream) and a difference (favorite flavor).

> ➤ **Review Video: Compare and Contrast**
> *Visit* **mometrix.com/academy** *and enter* **Code: 798319**

One of the most common text structures is **cause and effect**. A cause is an act or event that makes something happen, and an effect is the thing that happens as a result of that cause. A cause-and-effect relationship is not always explicit, but there are some words in English that signal causality, such as *since*, *because*, and *as a result*. As an example, consider the sentence *Because the sky was clear, Ron did not bring an umbrella*. The cause is the clear sky, and the effect is that Ron did not bring an umbrella. However, sometimes the cause-and-effect relationship will not be clearly noted. For instance, the sentence *He was late and missed the meeting* does not contain any signaling words, but it still contains a cause (he was late) and an effect (he missed the meeting). It is possible for a single cause to have multiple effects, or for a single effect to have multiple causes. Also, an effect can in turn be the cause of another effect, in what is known as a cause-and-effect chain.

Authors often use analogies to add meaning to the text. An **analogy** is a comparison of two things. The words in the analogy are connected by a certain, often undetermined relationship. Look at this analogy: moo is to cow as quack is to duck. This analogy compares the sound that a cow makes with the sound that a duck makes. Even if the word 'quack' was not given, one could figure out it is the correct word to complete the analogy based on the relationship between the words 'moo' and 'cow'. Some common relationships for analogies include synonyms, antonyms, part to whole, definition, and actor to action.

Another element that impacts a text is the author's point of view. The **point of view** of a text is the perspective from which it is told. The author will always have a point of view about a story before he draws up a plot line. The author will know what events they want to take place, how they want the characters to interact, and how the story will resolve. An author will also have an opinion on the topic, or series of events, which is presented in the story, based on their own prior experience and beliefs.

> ➢ **Review Video: Point of View**
> Visit **mometrix.com/academy** and enter **Code: 383336**

The two main points of view that authors use are first person and third person. If the narrator of the story is also the main character, or *protagonist*, the text is written in first-person point of view. In first person, the author writes with the word *I*. Third-person point of view is probably the most common point of view that authors use. Using third person, authors refer to each character using the words *he* or *she*. In third-person omniscient, the narrator is not a character in the story and tells the story of all of the characters at the same time.

A good writer will use **transitional words** and phrases to guide the reader through the text. You are no doubt familiar with the common transitions, though you may never have considered how they operate. Some transitional phrases (*after, before, during, in the middle of*) give information about time. Some indicate that an example is about to be given (*for example, in fact, for instance*). Writers use them to compare (*also, likewise*) and contrast (*however, but, yet*). Transitional words and phrases can suggest addition (*and, also, furthermore, moreover*) and logical relationships (*if, then, therefore, as a result, since*). Finally, transitional words and phrases can demarcate the steps in a process (*first, second, last*). You should incorporate transitional words and phrases where they will orient your reader and illuminate the structure of your composition.

Types of Passages

A **narrative** passage is a story. Narratives can be fiction or nonfiction. However, there are a few elements that a text must have in order to be classified as a narrative. To begin with, the text must have a plot. That is, it must describe a series of events. If it is a good narrative, these events will be interesting and emotionally engaging to the reader. A narrative also has characters. These could be people, animals, or even inanimate objects, so long as they participate in the plot. A narrative passage often contains figurative language, which is meant to stimulate the imagination of the reader by making comparisons and observations. A metaphor, which is a description of one thing in terms of another, is a common piece of figurative language. *The moon was a frosty snowball* is an example of a metaphor: it is obviously untrue in the literal sense, but it suggests a certain mood for the reader. Narratives often proceed in a clear sequence, but they do not need to do so.

An **expository** passage aims to inform and enlighten the reader. It is nonfiction and usually centers around a simple, easily defined topic. Since the goal of exposition is to teach, such a passage should be as clear as possible. It is common for an expository passage to contain helpful organizing words, like *first, next, for example*, and *therefore*. These words keep the reader oriented in the text. Although expository passages do not need to feature colorful language and artful writing, they are often more effective when they do. For a reader, the challenge of expository passages is to maintain steady attention. Expository passages are not always about subjects in which a reader will naturally be interested, and the writer is often more concerned with clarity and comprehensibility than with engaging the reader. For this reason, many expository passages are dull. Making notes is a good way to maintain focus when reading an expository passage.

A **technical** passage is written to describe a complex object or process. Technical writing is common in medical and technological fields, in which complicated mathematical, scientific, and engineering ideas need to be explained simply and clearly. To ease comprehension, a technical passage usually proceeds in a very logical order. Technical passages often have clear headings and subheadings, which are used to keep the reader oriented in the text. It is also common for these passages to break sections up with numbers or letters. Many technical passages look more like an outline than a piece of prose. The amount of jargon or difficult vocabulary will vary in a technical passage depending on the intended audience. As much as possible, technical passages try to avoid language that the reader will have to research in order to understand the message. Of course, it is not always possible to avoid jargon.

A **persuasive** passage is meant to change the reader's mind or lead her into agreement with the author. The persuasive intent may be obvious, or it may be quite difficult to discern. In some cases, a persuasive passage will be indistinguishable from an informative passage: it will make an assertion and offer supporting details. However, a persuasive passage is more likely to make claims based on opinion and to appeal to the reader's emotions. Persuasive passages may not describe alternate positions and, when they do, they often display significant bias. It may be clear that a persuasive passage is giving the author's viewpoint, or the passage may adopt a seemingly objective tone. A persuasive passage is successful if it can make a convincing argument and win the trust of the reader.

A persuasive essay will likely focus on one central argument, but it may make many smaller claims along the way. These are subordinate arguments with which the reader must agree if he or she is going to agree with the central argument. The central argument will only be as strong as the subordinate claims. These claims should be rooted in fact and observation, rather than subjective judgment. The best persuasive essays provide enough supporting detail to justify claims without overwhelming the reader. Remember that a fact must be susceptible to independent verification: that is, it must be something the reader could confirm. Also, statistics are only effective when they take into account possible objections. For instance, a statistic on the number of foreclosed houses would only be useful if it was taken over a defined interval and in a defined area. Most readers are wary of statistics, because they are so often misleading. If possible, a persuasive essay should always include references so that the reader can obtain more information. Of course, this means that the writer's accuracy and fairness may be judged by the inquiring reader.

Opinions are formed by emotion as well as reason, and persuasive writers often appeal to the feelings of the reader. Although readers should always be skeptical of this technique, it is often used in a proper and ethical manner. For instance, there are many subjects that have an obvious emotional component, and therefore cannot be completely treated without an appeal to the emotions. Consider an article on drunk driving: it makes sense to include some specific examples that will alarm or sadden the reader. After all, drunk driving often has serious and tragic consequences. Emotional appeals are not appropriate, however, when they attempt to mislead the reader. For instance, in political advertisements it is common to emphasize the patriotism of the preferred candidate, because this will encourage the audience to link their own positive feelings about the country with their opinion of the candidate. However, these ads often imply that the other candidate is unpatriotic, which in most cases is far from the truth. Another common and improper emotional appeal is the use of loaded language, as for instance referring to an avidly religious person as a "fanatic" or a passionate environmentalist as a "tree hugger." These terms introduce an emotional component that detracts from the argument.

History and Culture

Historical context has a profound influence on literature: the events, knowledge base, and assumptions of an author's time color every aspect of his or her work. Sometimes, authors hold opinions and use language that would be considered inappropriate or immoral in a modern setting, but that was acceptable in the author's time. As a reader, one should consider how the historical context influenced a work and also how today's opinions and ideas shape the way modern readers read the works of the past. For instance, in most societies of the past, women were treated as second-class citizens. An author who wrote in 18th-century England might sound sexist to modern readers, even if that author was relatively feminist in his time. Readers should not have to excuse the faulty assumptions and prejudices of the past, but they should appreciate that a person's thoughts and words are, in part, a result of the time and culture in which they live or lived, and it is perhaps unfair to expect writers to avoid all of the errors of their times.

> ➢ **Review Video: Historical Context**
> *Visit **momentrix.com/academy** and enter **Code: 169770***

Even a brief study of world literature suggests that writers from vastly different cultures address similar themes. For instance, works like the *Odyssey* and *Hamlet* both tackle the individual's battle for self-control and independence. In every culture, authors address themes of personal growth and the struggle for maturity. Another universal theme is the conflict between the individual and society. In works as culturally disparate as *Native Son*, the *Aeneid*, and *1984*, authors dramatize how people struggle to maintain their personalities and dignity in large, sometimes oppressive groups. Finally, many cultures have versions of the hero's (or heroine's) journey, in which an adventurous person must overcome many obstacles in order to gain greater knowledge, power, and perspective. Some famous works that treat this theme are the *Epic of Gilgamesh*, Dante's *Divine Comedy*, and *Don Quixote*.

Authors from different genres (for instance poetry, drama, novel, short story) and cultures may address similar themes, but they often do so quite differently. For instance, poets are likely to address subject matter obliquely, through the use of images and allusions. In a play, on the other hand, the author is more likely to dramatize themes by using characters to express opposing viewpoints. This disparity is known as a dialectical approach. In a novel, the author does not need to express themes directly; rather, they can be illustrated through events and actions. In some regional literatures, like those of Greece or England, authors use more irony: their works have characters that express views and make decisions that are clearly disapproved of by the author. In Latin America, there is a great tradition of using supernatural events to illustrate themes about real life. In China and Japan, authors frequently use well-established regional forms (haiku, for instance) to organize their treatment of universal themes.

Responding to Literature

When reading good literature, the reader is moved to engage actively in the text. One part of being an active reader involves making predictions. A **prediction** is a guess about what will happen next. Readers are constantly making predictions based on what they have read and what they already know. Consider the following sentence: *Staring at the computer screen in shock, Kim blindly reached over for the brimming glass of water on the shelf to her side.* The sentence suggests that Kim is agitated and that she is not looking at the glass she is going to pick up, so a reader might predict that she is going to knock the glass over. Of course, not every prediction will be accurate: perhaps Kim will pick the glass up cleanly. Nevertheless, the author has certainly created the expectation that the water might be spilled. Predictions are always subject to revision as the reader acquires more information.

Test-taking tip: To respond to questions requiring future predictions, the student's answers should be based on evidence of past or present behavior.

Readers are often required to understand text that claims and suggests ideas without stating them directly. An **inference** is a piece of information that is implied but not written outright by the author. For instance, consider the following sentence: *Mark made more money that week than he had in the previous year.* From this sentence, the reader can infer that Mark either has not made much money in the previous year or made a great deal of money that week. Often, a reader can use information he or she already knows to make inferences. Take as an example the sentence *When his coffee arrived, he looked around the table for the silver cup.* Many people know that cream is typically served in a silver cup, so using their own base of knowledge they can infer that the subject of this sentence takes his coffee with cream. Making inferences requires concentration, attention, and practice.

Test-taking tip: While being tested on his ability to make correct inferences, the student must look for contextual clues. An answer can be *true* but not *correct*. The contextual clues will help you find the answer that is the best answer out of the given choices. Understand the context in which a phrase is stated. When asked for the implied meaning of a statement made in the passage, the student should immediately locate the statement and read the context in which it was made. Also, look for an answer choice that has a similar phrase to the statement in question.

A reader must be able to identify a text's **sequence**, or the order in which things happen. Often, and especially when the sequence is very important to the author, it is indicated with signal words like *first*, *then*, *next*, and *last*. However, sometimes a sequence is merely implied and must be noted by the reader. Consider the sentence *He walked in the front door and switched on the hall lamp.* Clearly, the man did not turn the lamp on before he walked in the door, so the implied sequence is that he first walked in the door and then turned on the lamp. Texts do not always proceed in an orderly sequence from first to last: sometimes, they begin at the end and then start over at the beginning. As a reader, it can be useful to make brief notes to clarify the sequence.

In addition to inferring and predicting things about the text, the reader must often **draw conclusions** about the information he has read. When asked for a *conclusion* that may be drawn, look for critical "hedge" phrases, such as *likely*, *may*, *can*, *will often*, among many others. When you are being tested on this knowledge, remember that question writers insert these hedge phrases to cover every possibility. Often an answer will be wrong simply because it leaves no room for exception. Extreme positive or negative answers (such as always, never, etc.) are usually not correct. The reader should not use any outside knowledge that is not gathered from the reading passage to answer the related questions. Correct answers can be derived straight from the reading passage.

Literary Genres

Literary genres refer to the basic generic types of poetry, drama, fiction, and nonfiction. Literary genre is a method of classifying and analyzing literature. There are numerous subdivisions within genre, including such categories as novels, novellas, and short stories in fiction. Drama may also be subdivided into comedy, tragedy, and many other categories. Poetry and nonfiction have their own distinct divisions.

Genres often overlap, and the distinctions among them are blurred, such as that between the nonfiction novel and docudrama, as well as many others. However, the use of genres is helpful to the reader as a set of understandings that guide our responses to a work. The generic norm sets expectations and forms the framework within which we read and evaluate a work. This framework will guide both our understanding and interpretation of the work. It is a useful tool for both literary criticism and analysis.

Fiction is a general term for any form of literary narrative that is invented or imagined rather than being factual. For those individuals who equate fact with truth, the imagined or invented character of fiction tends to render it relatively unimportant or trivial among the genres. Defenders of fiction are quick to point out that the fictional mode is an essential part of being. The ability to imagine or discuss what-if plots, characters, and events is clearly part of the human experience.

Prose is derived from the Latin and means "straightforward discourse." Prose fiction, although having many categories, may be divided into three main groups:

- **Short stories**: a fictional narrative, the length of which varies, usually under 20,000 words. Short stories usually have only a few characters and generally describe one major event or insight. The short story began in magazines in the late 1800s and has flourished ever since.

- **Novels**: a longer work of fiction, often containing a large cast of characters and extensive plotting. The emphasis may be on an event, action, social problems, or any experience. There is now a genre of nonfiction novels pioneered by Truman Capote's *In Cold Blood* in the 1960s. Novels may also be written in verse.

- **Novellas**: a work of narrative fiction longer than a short story but shorter than a novel. Novellas may also be called short novels or novelettes. They originated from the German tradition and have become common forms in all of the world's literature.

Many elements influence a work of prose fiction. Some important ones are:

- Speech and dialogue: Characters may speak for themselves or through the narrator. Dialogue may be realistic or fantastic, depending on the author's aim.

- Thoughts and mental processes: There may be internal dialogue used as a device for plot development or character understanding.

- Dramatic involvement: Some narrators encourage readers to become involved in the events of the story, whereas others attempt to distance readers through literary devices.

- Action: This is any information that advances the plot or involves new interactions between the characters.

- Duration: The time frame of the work may be long or short, and the relationship between described time and narrative time may vary.

- Setting and description: Is the setting critical to the plot or characters? How are the action scenes described?

- Themes: This is any point of view or topic given sustained attention.

- Symbolism: Authors often veil meanings through imagery and other literary constructions.

Fiction is much wider than simply prose fiction. Songs, ballads, epics, and narrative poems are examples of non-prose fiction. A full definition of fiction must include not only the work itself but also the framework in which it is read. Literary fiction can also be defined as not true rather than nonexistent, as many works of historical fiction refer to real people, places, and events that are treated imaginatively as if they were true. These imaginary elements enrich and broaden literary expression.

When analyzing fiction, it is important for the reader to look carefully at the work being studied. The plot or action of a narrative can become so entertaining that the language of the work is ignored. The language of fiction should not simply be a way to relate a plot—it should also yield many insights to the judicious reader. Some prose fiction is based on the reader's engagement with the language rather than the story. A studious reader will analyze the mode of expression as well as the narrative. Part of the reward of reading in this manner is to discover how the author uses different language to describe familiar objects, events, or emotions. Some works focus the reader on an author's unorthodox use of language, whereas others may emphasize characters or storylines. What happens in a story is not always the critical element in the work. This type of reading may be difficult at first but yields great rewards.

> ➤ **Review Video: Reading Fiction**
> Visit **mometrix.com/academy** and enter **Code: 391411**

The **narrator** is a central part of any work of fiction, and can give insight about the purpose of the work and its main themes and ideas. The following are important questions to address to better understand the voice and role of the narrator and incorporate that voice into an overall understanding of the novel:
- Who is the narrator of the novel? What is the narrator's perspective, first person or third person? What is the role of the narrator in the plot? Are there changes in narrators or the perspective of narrators?

- Does the narrator explain things in the novel, or does meaning emerge from the plot and events? The personality of the narrator is important. She may have a vested interest in a character or event described. Some narratives follow the time sequence of the plot, whereas others do not. A narrator may express approval or disapproval about a character or events in the work.

- Tone is an important aspect of the narration. Who is actually being addressed by the narrator? Is the tone familiar or formal, intimate or impersonal? Does the vocabulary suggest clues about the narrator?

A **character** is a person intimately involved with the plot and development of the novel. Development of the novel's characters not only moves the story along but will also tell the reader a lot about the novel itself. There is usually a physical description of the character, but this is often omitted in modern and postmodern novels. These works may focus on the psychological state or motivation of the character. The choice of a character's name may give valuable clues to his role in the work.

Characters are said to be flat or round. Flat characters tend to be minor figures in the story, changing little or not at all. Round characters (those understood from a well-rounded view) are more central to the story and tend to change as the plot unfolds. Stock characters are similar to flat characters, filling out the story without influencing it.

Modern literature has been greatly affected by Freudian psychology, giving rise to such devices as the interior monologue and magical realism as methods of understanding characters in a work. These give the reader a more complex understanding of the inner lives of the characters and enrich the understanding of relationships between characters.

Another important genre is that of **drama**: a play written to be spoken aloud. The drama is in many ways inseparable from performance. Reading drama ideally involves using imagination to visualize and re-create the play with characters and settings. The reader stages the play in his imagination, watching characters interact and developments unfold. Sometimes this involves simulating a theatrical presentation; other times it involves imagining the events. In either case, the reader is imagining the unwritten to re-create the dramatic experience. Novels present some of the same problems, but a narrator will provide much more information about the setting, characters, inner dialogues, and many other supporting details. In drama, much of this is missing, and we are required to use our powers of projection and imagination to taste the full flavor of the dramatic work. There are many empty spaces in dramatic texts that must be filled by the reader to fully appreciate the work.

When reading drama in this way, there are some advantages over watching the play performed (though there is much criticism in this regard):

- Freedom of point of view and perspective: Text is free of interpretations of actors, directors, producers, and technical staging.

- Additional information: The text of a drama may be accompanied by notes or prefaces placing the work in a social or historical context. Stage directions may also provide relevant information about the author's purpose. None of this is typically available at live or filmed performances.

- Study and understanding: Difficult or obscure passages may be studied at leisure and supplemented by explanatory works. This is particularly true of older plays with unfamiliar language, which cannot be fully understood without an opportunity to study the material.

Critical elements of drama, especially when it is being read aloud or performed, include dialect, speech, and dialogue. Analysis of speech and dialogue is important in the critical study of drama. Some playwrights use speech to develop their characters. Speeches may be long or short, and written in as normal prose or blank verse. Some characters have a unique way of speaking which illuminates aspects of the drama. Emphasis and tone are both important, as well. Does the author make clear the tone in which lines are to be spoken, or is this open to interpretation? Sometimes there are various possibilities in tone with regard to delivering lines.

Dialect is any distinct variety of a language, especially one spoken in a region or part of a country. The criterion for distinguishing dialects from languages is that of mutual understanding. For example, people who speak Dutch cannot understand English unless they have learned it. But a speaker from Amsterdam can understand one from Antwerp; therefore, they speak different dialects of the same language. This is, however, a matter of degree; there are languages in which different dialects are unintelligible.

Dialect mixtures are the presence in one form of speech with elements from different neighboring dialects. The study of speech differences from one geographical area to another is called dialect geography. A dialect atlas is a map showing distribution of dialects in a given area. A dialect continuum shows a progressive shift in dialects across a territory, such that adjacent dialects are understandable, but those at the extremes are not.

Dramatic dialogue can be difficult to interpret and changes depending upon the tone used and which words are emphasized. Where the stresses, or meters, of dramatic dialogue fall can determine meaning. Variations in emphasis are only one factor in the manipulability of dramatic speech. Tone is of equal or greater importance and expresses a range of possible emotions and feelings that cannot be readily discerned from the script of a play. The reader must add tone to the words to understand the full meaning of a passage. Recognizing tone is a cumulative process as the reader begins to understand the characters and situations in the play. Other elements that influence the interpretation of dialogue include the setting, possible reactions of the characters to the speech, and possible gestures or facial expressions of the actor. There are no firm rules to guide the interpretation of dramatic speech. An open and flexible attitude is essential in interpreting dramatic dialogue.

Action is a crucial element in the production of a dramatic work. Many dramas contain little dialogue and much action. In these cases, it is essential for the reader to carefully study stage directions and visualize the action on the stage. Benefits of understanding stage directions include knowing which characters are on the stage at all times, who is speaking to whom, and following these patterns through changes of scene.

Stage directions also provide additional information, some of which is not available to a live audience. The nature of the physical space where the action occurs is vital, and stage directions help with this. The historical context of the period is important in understanding what the playwright was working with in terms of theaters and physical space. The type of staging possible for the author is a good guide to the spatial elements of a production.

Asides and soliloquies are devices that authors use in plot and character development. **Asides** indicate that not all characters are privy to the lines. This may be a method of advancing or explaining the plot in a subtle manner. **Soliloquies** are opportunities for character development, plot enhancement, and to give insight to characters motives, feelings, and emotions. Careful study of these elements provides a reader with an abundance of clues to the major themes and plot of the work.

Art, music, and literature all interact in ways that contain many opportunities for the enrichment of all of the arts. Students could apply their knowledge of art and music by creating illustrations for a work or creating a musical score for a text. Students could discuss the meanings of texts and decide on their illustrations, or a score could amplify the meaning of the text.

Understanding the art and music of a period can make the experience of literature a richer, more rewarding experience. Students should be encouraged to use the knowledge of art and music to illuminate the text. Examining examples of dress, architecture, music, and dance of a period may be helpful in a fuller engagement of the text. Much of period literature lends itself to the analysis of the prevailing taste in art and music of an era, which helps place the literary work in a more meaningful context.

Critical Thinking Skills

Opinions, Facts, & Fallacies
Critical thinking skills are mastered through understanding various types of writing and the different purposes that authors have for writing the way they do. Every author writes for a purpose. Understanding that purpose, and how they accomplish their goal, will allow you to critique the writing and determine whether or not you agree with their conclusions.

Readers must always be conscious of the distinction between fact and opinion. A **fact** can be subjected to analysis and can be either proved or disproved. An **opinion**, on the other hand, is the author's personal feeling, which may not be alterable by research, evidence, or argument. If the author writes that the distance from New York to Boston is about two hundred miles, he is stating a fact. But if he writes that New York is too crowded, then he is giving an opinion, because there is no objective standard for overpopulation. An opinion may be indicated by words like *believe*, *think*, or *feel*. Also, an opinion may be supported by facts: for instance, the author might give the population density of New York as a reason for why it is overcrowded. An opinion supported by fact tends to be more convincing. When authors support their opinions with other opinions, the reader is unlikely to be moved.

Facts should be presented to the reader from reliable sources. An opinion is what the author thinks about a given topic. An opinion is not common knowledge or proven by expert sources, but it is information that the author believes and wants the reader to consider. To distinguish between fact and opinion, a reader needs to look at the type of source that is presenting information, what information backs-up a claim, and whether or not the author may be motivated to have a certain point of view on a given topic. For example, if a panel of scientists has conducted multiple studies on the effectiveness of taking a certain vitamin, the results are more likely to be factual than if a company selling a vitamin claims that taking the vitamin can produce positive effects. The company is motivated to sell its product, while the scientists are using the scientific method to prove a theory. If the author uses words such as "I think…", the statement is an opinion.

In their attempt to persuade, writers often make mistakes in their thinking patterns and writing choices. It's important to understand these so you can make an informed decision. Every author has a point of view, but when an author ignores reasonable counterarguments or distorts opposing viewpoints, she is demonstrating a **bias**. A bias is evident whenever the author is unfair or inaccurate in his or her presentation. Bias may be intentional or unintentional, but it should always alert the reader to be skeptical of the argument being made. It should be noted that a biased author may still be correct. However, the author will be correct in spite of her bias, not because of it. A **stereotype** is like a bias, except that it is specifically applied to a group or place. Stereotyping is considered to be particularly abhorrent because it promotes negative generalizations about people. Many people are familiar with some of the hateful stereotypes of certain ethnic, religious, and cultural groups. Readers should be very wary of authors who stereotype. These faulty assumptions typically reveal the author's ignorance and lack of curiosity.

Sometimes, authors will **appeal to the reader's emotion** in an attempt to persuade or to distract the reader from the weakness of the argument. For instance, the author may try to inspire the pity of the reader by delivering a heart-rending story. An author also might use the bandwagon approach, in which he suggests that his opinion is correct because it is held by the majority. Some authors resort to name-calling, in which insults and harsh words are delivered to the opponent in an attempt to distract. In advertising, a common appeal is the testimonial, in which a famous person endorses a product. Of course, the fact that a celebrity likes something should not really mean anything to the reader. These and other emotional appeals are usually evidence of poor reasoning and a weak argument.

Certain *logical fallacies* are frequent in writing. A logical fallacy is a failure of reasoning. As a reader, it is important to recognize logical fallacies, because they diminish the value of the author's message. The four most common logical fallacies in writing are the false analogy, circular reasoning, false dichotomy, and overgeneralization. In a **false analogy**, the author suggests that two things are similar, when in fact they are different. This fallacy is often committed when the author is attempting to convince the reader that something unknown is like something relatively familiar. The author takes advantage of the reader's ignorance to make this false comparison. One example might be the following statement: *Failing to tip a waitress is like stealing money out of somebody's wallet.* Of course, failing to tip is very rude, especially when the service has been good, but people are not arrested for failing to tip as they would for stealing money from a wallet. To compare stingy diners with thieves is a false analogy.

Circular reasoning is one of the more difficult logical fallacies to identify, because it is typically hidden behind dense language and complicated sentences. Reasoning is described as circular when it offers no support for assertions other than restating them in different words. Put another way, a circular argument refers to itself as evidence of truth. A simple example of circular argument is when a person uses a word to define itself, such as saying *Niceness is the state of being nice.* If the reader does not know what *nice* means, then this definition will not be very useful. In a text, circular reasoning is usually more complex. For instance, an author might say *Poverty is a problem for society because it creates trouble for people throughout the community.* It is redundant to say that poverty is a problem because it creates trouble. When an author engages in circular reasoning, it is often because he or she has not fully thought out the argument, or cannot come up with any legitimate justifications.

One of the most common logical fallacies is the **false dichotomy**, in which the author creates an artificial sense that there are only two possible alternatives in a situation. This fallacy is common when the author has an agenda and wants to give the impression that his view is the only sensible one. A false dichotomy has the effect of limiting the reader's options and imagination. An example of a false dichotomy is the statement *You need to go to the party with me, otherwise you'll just be bored at home.* The speaker suggests that the only other possibility besides being at the party is being bored at home. But this is not true, as it is perfectly possible to be entertained at home, or even to go somewhere other than the party. Readers should always be wary of the false dichotomy: when an author limits alternatives, it is always wise to ask whether he is being valid.

Overgeneralization is a logical fallacy in which the author makes a claim that is so broad it cannot be proved or disproved. In most cases, overgeneralization occurs when the author wants to create an illusion of authority, or when he is using sensational language to sway the opinion of the reader. For instance, in the sentence *Everybody knows that she is a terrible teacher*, the author makes an assumption that cannot really be believed. This kind of statement is made when the author wants to create the illusion of consensus when none actually exists: it may be that most people have a negative view of the teacher, but to say that *everybody* feels that way is an exaggeration. When a reader spots overgeneralization, she should become skeptical about the argument that is being made, because an author will often try to hide a weak or unsupported assertion behind authoritative language.

Two other types of logical fallacies are **slippery slope** arguments and **hasty generalizations**. In a slippery slope argument, the author says that if something happens, it automatically means that something else will happen as a result, even though this may not be true. (i.e., just because you study hard does not mean you are going to ace the test). "Hasty generalization" is drawing a conclusion too early, without finishing analyzing the details of the argument. Writers of persuasive texts often use these techniques because they are very effective. In order to **identify logical fallacies**, readers need to read carefully and ask questions as they read. Thinking critically means not taking everything at face value. Readers need to critically evaluate an author's argument to make sure that the logic used is sound.

Organization of the Text
The way a text is organized can help the reader to understand more clearly the author's intent and his conclusions. There are various ways to organize a text, and each one has its own purposes and uses.

Some nonfiction texts are organized to **present a problem** followed by a solution. In this type of text, it is common for the problem to be explained before the solution is offered. In some cases, as when the problem is well known, the solution may be briefly introduced at the beginning. The entire passage may focus on the solution, and the problem will be referenced only occasionally. Some texts will outline multiple solutions to a problem, leaving the reader to choose among them. If the author has an interest or an allegiance to one solution, he may fail to mention or may describe inaccurately some of the other solutions. Readers should be careful of the author's agenda when reading a problem-solution text. Only by understanding the author's point of view and interests can one develop a proper judgment of the proposed solution.

Authors need to organize information logically so the reader can follow it and locate information within the text. Two common organizational structures are cause and effect and chronological order. When using **chronological order**, the author presents information in the order that it happened. For example, biographies are written in chronological order; the subject's birth and childhood are presented first, followed by their adult life, and lastly by the events leading up to the person's death.

In **cause and effect**, an author presents one thing that makes something else happen. For example, if one were to go to bed very late, they would be tired. The cause is going to bed late, with the effect of being tired the next day.

It can be tricky to identify the cause-and-effect relationships in a text, but there are a few ways to approach this task. To begin with, these relationships are often signaled with certain terms. When an author uses words like *because, since, in order*, and *so*, she is likely describing a cause-and-effect relationship. Consider the sentence, "He called her because he needed the homework." This is a simple causal relationship, in which the cause was his need for the homework and the effect was his phone call. Not all cause-and-effect relationships are marked in this way, however. Consider the sentences, "He called her. He needed the homework." When the cause-and-effect relationship is not indicated with a keyword, it can be discovered by asking why something happened. He called her: why? The answer is in the next sentence: He needed the homework.

Persuasive essays, in which an author tries to make a convincing argument and change the reader's mind, usually include cause-and-effect relationships. However, these relationships should not always be taken at face value. An author frequently will assume a cause or take an effect for granted. To read a persuasive essay effectively, one needs to judge the cause-and-effect relationships the author is presenting. For instance, imagine an author wrote the following: "The parking deck has been unprofitable because people would prefer to ride their bikes." The relationship is clear: the cause is that people prefer to ride their bikes, and the effect is that the parking deck has been unprofitable. However, a reader should consider whether this argument is conclusive. Perhaps there are other reasons for the failure of the parking deck: a down economy, excessive fees, etc. Too often, authors present causal relationships as if they are fact rather than opinion. Readers should be on the alert for these dubious claims.

Thinking critically about ideas and conclusions can seem like a daunting task. One way to make it easier is to understand the basic elements of ideas and writing techniques. Looking at the way different ideas relate to each other can be a good way for the reader to begin his analysis. For instance, sometimes writers will write about two different ideas that are in opposition to each other. The analysis of these opposing ideas is known as **contrast**. Contrast is often marred by the author's obvious partiality to one of the ideas. A discerning reader will be put off by an author who does not engage in a fair fight. In an analysis of opposing ideas, both ideas should be presented in their clearest and most reasonable terms. If the author does prefer a side, he should avoid indicating this preference with pejorative language. An analysis of opposing ideas should proceed through the major differences point by point, with a full explanation of each side's view. For instance, in an analysis of capitalism and communism, it would be important to outline each side's view on labor, markets, prices, personal responsibility, etc. It would be less effective to describe the theory of communism and then explain how capitalism has thrived in the West. An analysis of opposing views should present each side in the same manner.

Many texts follow the **compare-and-contrast** model, in which the similarities and differences between two ideas or things are explored. Analysis of the similarities between ideas is called comparison. In order for a comparison to work, the author must place the ideas or things in an equivalent structure. That is, the author must present the ideas in the same way. Imagine an author wanted to show the similarities between cricket and baseball. The correct way to do so would be to summarize the equipment and rules for each game. It would be incorrect to summarize the equipment of cricket and then lay out the history of baseball, since this would make it impossible for the reader to see the similarities. It is perhaps too obvious to say that an analysis of similar ideas should emphasize the similarities. Of course, the author should take care to include any differences that must be mentioned. Often, these small differences will only reinforce the more general similarity.

Drawing Conclusions

Authors should have a clear purpose in mind while writing. Especially when reading informational texts, it is important to understand the logical conclusion of the author's ideas. **Identifying this logical conclusion** can help the reader understand whether he agrees with the writer or not. Identifying a logical conclusion is much like making an inference: it requires the reader to combine the information given by the text with what he already knows to make a supportable assertion. If a passage is written well, then the conclusion should be obvious even when it is unstated. If the author intends the reader to draw a certain conclusion, then all of his argumentation and detail should be leading toward it. One way to approach the task of drawing conclusions is to make brief notes of all the points made by the author. When these are arranged on paper, they may clarify the logical conclusion. Another way to approach conclusions is to consider whether the reasoning of the author raises any pertinent questions. Sometimes it will be possible to draw several conclusions from a passage, and on occasion these will be conclusions that were never imagined by the author. It is essential, however, that these conclusions be supported directly by the text.

The term **text evidence** refers to information that supports a main point or points in a story, and can help lead the reader to a conclusion. Information used as *text evidence* is precise, descriptive, and factual. A main point is often followed by supporting details that provide evidence to back-up a claim. For example, a story may include the claim that winter occurs during opposite months in the Northern and Southern hemispheres. *Text evidence* based on this claim may include countries where winter occurs in opposite months, along with reasons that winter occurs at different times of the year in separate hemispheres (due to the tilt of the Earth as it rotates around the sun).

Readers interpret text and respond to it in a number of ways. Using textual support helps defend your response or interpretation because it roots your thinking in the text. You are interpreting based on information in the text and not simply your own ideas. When crafting a response, look for important quotes and details from the text to help bolster your argument. If you are writing about a character's personality trait, for example, use details from the text to show that the character acted in such a way. You can also include statistics and facts from a nonfiction text to strengthen your response. For example, instead of writing, "A lot of people use cell phones," use statistics to provide the exact number. This strengthens your argument because it is more precise.

The text used to support an argument can be the argument's downfall if it is not credible. A text is **credible**, or believable, when the author is knowledgeable and objective, or unbiased. The author's motivations for writing the text play a critical role in determining the credibility of the text and must be evaluated when assessing that credibility. The author's motives should be for the dissemination of information. The purpose of the text should be to inform or describe, not to persuade. When an author writes a persuasive text, he has the motivation that the reader will do what they want. The extent of the author's knowledge of the topic and their motivation must be evaluated when assessing the credibility of a text. Reports written about the Ozone layer by an environmental scientist and a hairdresser will have a different level of credibility.

After determining your own opinion and evaluating the credibility of your supporting text, it is sometimes necessary to communicate your ideas and findings to others. When **writing a response to a text**, it is important to use elements of the text to support your assertion or defend your position. Using supporting evidence from the text strengthens the argument because the reader can see how in depth the writer read the original piece and based their response on the details and facts within that text. Elements of text that can be used in a response include: facts, details, statistics, and direct quotations from the text. When writing a response, one must make sure they indicate which information comes from the original text and then base their discussion, argument, or defense around this information.

A reader should always be drawing conclusions from the text. Sometimes conclusions are implied from written information, and other times the information is **stated directly** within the passage. It is always more comfortable to draw conclusions from information stated within a passage, rather than to draw them from mere implications. At times an author may provide some information and then describe a counterargument. The reader should be alert for direct statements that are subsequently rejected or weakened by the author. The reader should always read the entire passage before drawing conclusions. Many readers are trained to expect the author's conclusions at either the beginning or the end of the passage, but many texts do not adhere to this format.

Drawing conclusions from information implied within a passage requires confidence on the part of the reader. **Implications** are things the author does not state directly, but which can be assumed based on what the author does say. For instance, consider the following simple passage: "I stepped outside and opened my umbrella. By the time I got to work, the cuffs of my pants were soaked." The author never states that it is raining, but this fact is clearly implied. Conclusions based on implication must be well supported by the text. In order to draw a solid conclusion, a reader should have multiple pieces of evidence, or, if he only has one, must be assured that there is no other possible explanation than his conclusion. A good reader will be able to draw many conclusions from information implied by the text, which enriches the reading experience considerably.

As an aid to drawing conclusions, the reader should be adept at **outlining** the information contained in the passage; an effective outline will reveal the structure of the passage, and will lead to solid conclusions. An effective outline will have a title that refers to the basic subject of the text, though it need not recapitulate the main idea. In most outlines, the main idea will be the first major section. It will have each major idea of the passage established as the head of a category. For instance, the most common outline format calls for the main ideas of the passage to be indicated with Roman numerals. In an effective outline of this kind, each of the main ideas will be represented by a Roman numeral and none of the Roman numerals will designate minor details or secondary ideas. Moreover, all supporting ideas and details should be placed in the appropriate place on the outline. An outline does not need to include every detail listed in the text, but it should feature all of those that are central to the argument or message. Each of these details should be listed under the appropriate main idea.

It is also helpful to **summarize** the information you have read in a paragraph or passage format. This process is similar to creating an effective outline. To begin with, a summary should accurately define the main idea of the passage, though it does not need to explain this main idea in exhaustive detail. It should continue by laying out the most important supporting details or arguments from the passage. All of the significant supporting details should be included, and none of the details included should be irrelevant or insignificant. Also, the summary should accurately report all of these details. Too often, the desire for brevity in a summary leads to the sacrifice of clarity or veracity. Summaries are often difficult to read, because they omit all of graceful language, digressions, and asides that distinguish great writing. However, if the summary is effective, it should contain much the same message as the original text.

Paraphrasing is another method the reader can use to aid in comprehension. When paraphrasing, one puts what they have read into their own words, rephrasing what the author has written to make it their own, to "translate" all of what the author says to their own words, including as many details as they can.

Skimming

Your first task when you begin reading is to answer the question "What is the topic of the selection?" This can best be answered by quickly skimming the passage for the general idea, stopping to read only the first sentence of each paragraph. A paragraph's first is usually the main topic sentence, and it gives you a summary of the content of the paragraph.

Once you've skimmed the passage, stopping to read only the first sentences, you will have a general idea about what it is about, as well as what is the expected topic in each paragraph.

Each question will contain clues as to where to find the answer in the passage. Do not just randomly search through the passage for the correct answer to each question. Search scientifically. Find key word(s) or ideas in the question that are going to either contain or be near the correct answer. These are typically nouns, verbs, numbers, or phrases in the question that will probably be duplicated in the passage. Once you have identified those key word(s) or idea, skim the passage quickly to find where those key word(s) or idea appears. The correct answer choice will be nearby. *Example*:

What caused Martin to suddenly return to Paris?

The key word is Paris. Skim the passage quickly to find where this word appears. The answer will be close by that word.

However, sometimes key words in the question are not repeated in the passage. In those cases, search for the general idea of the question.

Example:

> Which of the following was the psychological impact of the author's childhood upon the remainder of his life?

Key words are "childhood" or "psychology". While searching for those words, be alert for other words or phrases that have similar meaning, such as "emotional effect" or "mentally" which could be used in the passage, rather than the exact word "psychology".

Numbers or years can be particularly good key words to skim for, as they stand out from the rest of the text.

Example:

> Which of the following best describes the influence of Monet's work in the 20th century?

20th contains numbers and will easily stand out from the rest of the text. Use 20th as the key word to skim for in the passage.

Other good key word(s) may be in quotation marks. These identify a word or phrase that is copied directly from the passage. In those cases, the word(s) in quotation marks are exactly duplicated in the passage.

Example:

> In her college years, what was meant by Margaret's "drive for excellence"?

"Drive for excellence" is a direct quote from the passage and should be easy to find.

Once you've quickly found the correct section of the passage to find the answer, focus upon the answer choices. Sometimes a choice will repeat word for word a portion of the passage near the answer. However, beware of such duplication – it may be a trap! More than likely, the correct choice will paraphrase or summarize the related portion of the passage, rather than being exactly the same wording.

For the answers that you think are correct, read them carefully and make sure that they answer the question. An answer can be factually correct, but it MUST answer the question asked. Additionally, two answers can both be seemingly correct, so be sure to read all of the answer choices, and make sure that you get the one that BEST answers the question.

Some questions will not have a key word:

Example:

> Which of the following would the author of this passage likely agree with?

In these cases, look for key words in the answer choices. Then skim the passage to find where the answer choice occurs. By skimming to find where to look, you can minimize the time required.

Sometimes it may be difficult to identify a good key word in the question to skim for in the passage. In those cases, look for a key word in one of the answer choices to skim for. Often the answer choices can all be found in the same paragraph, which can quickly narrow your search.

Paragraph focus

Focus upon the first sentence of each paragraph, which is the most important. The main topic of the paragraph is usually there.

Once you've read the first sentence in the paragraph, you have a general idea about what each paragraph will be about. As you read the questions, try to determine which paragraph will have the answer. Paragraphs have a concise topic. The answer should either obviously be there or obviously not. It will save time if you can jump straight to the paragraph, so try to remember what you learned from the first sentences.

Example:
> The first paragraph is about poets; the second is about poetry. If a question asks about poetry, where will the answer be? The second paragraph.

The main idea of a passage is typically spread across all or most of its paragraphs. Whereas the main idea of a paragraph may be completely different than the main idea of the very next paragraph, a main idea for a passage affects all of the paragraphs in one form or another.
Example:
> What is the main idea of the passage?

For each answer choice, try to see how many paragraphs are related. It can help to count how many sentences are affected by each choice, but it is best to see how many paragraphs are affected by the choice. Typically the answer choices will include incorrect choices that are main ideas of individual paragraphs, but not the entire passage. That is why it is crucial to choose ideas that are supported by the most paragraphs possible.

Eliminate choices

Some choices can quickly be eliminated. "Andy Warhol lived there." Is Andy Warhol even mentioned in the article? If not, quickly eliminate it.

When trying to answer a question such as "the passage indicates all of the following except" quickly skim the paragraph searching for references to each choice. If the reference exists, scratch it off as a choice. Similar choices may be crossed off simultaneously if they are close enough.

In choices that ask you to choose "which answer choice does NOT describe?" or "all of the following answer choices are identifiable characteristics, EXCEPT which?" look for answers that are similarly worded. Since only one answer can be correct, if there are two answers that appear to mean the same thing, they must BOTH be incorrect, and can be eliminated.

Example:

      A.)   changing values and attitudes

      B.)   a large population of mobile or uprooted people

These answer choices are similar; they both describe a fluid culture. Because of their similarity, they can be linked together. Since the answer can have only one choice, they can also be eliminated together.

When presented with a question that offers two choices, or neither choice, or both choice, it is rarely both choices.

Example:

When an atom emits a beta particle, the mass of the atom will:

      A.   increase

      B.   decrease.

      C.   stay the same.

      D.   either increase or decrease depending on conditions.

Answer D will rarely be correct, the answers are usually more concrete.

Contextual clues

Look for contextual clues. An answer can be right but not correct. The contextual clues will help you find the answer that is most right and is correct. Understand the context in which a phrase is stated.

When asked for the implied meaning of a statement made in the passage, immediately go find the statement and read the context it was made in. Also, look for an answer choice that has a similar phrase to the statement in question.

Example: In the passage, what is implied by the phrase "Churches have become more or less part of the furniture"?

Find an answer choice that is similar or describes the phrase "part of the furniture" as that is the key phrase in the question. "Part of the furniture" is a saying that means something is fixed, immovable, or set in their ways. Those are all similar ways of saying "part of the furniture." As such, the correct answer choice will probably include a similar rewording of the expression.

Example:

Why was John described as "morally desperate".

The answer will probably have some sort of definition of morals in it. "Morals" refers to a code of right and wrong behavior, so the correct answer choice will likely have words that mean something like that.

Fact/opinion

When asked about which statement is a fact or opinion, remember that answer choices that are facts will typically have no ambiguous words. For example, how long is a long time? What defines an ordinary person? These ambiguous words of "long" and "ordinary" should not be in a factual statement. However, if all of the choices have ambiguous words, go to the context of the passage. Often a factual statement may be set out as a research finding.
Example:
> "The scientist found that the eye reacts quickly to change in light."

Opinions may be set out in the context of words like thought, believed, understood, or wished.
Example:
> "He thought the Yankees should win the World Series."

Opposites

Answer choices that are direct opposites are usually correct. The paragraph will often contain established relationships (when this goes up, that goes down). The question may ask you to draw conclusions for this and will give two similar answer choices that are opposites.
Example:
> A.) if other factors are held constant, then increasing the interest rate will lead to a decrease in housing starts
> B.) if other factors are held constant, then increasing the interest rate will lead to an increase in housing starts

Often these opposites will not be so clearly recognized. Don't be thrown off by different wording, look for the meaning beneath. Notice how these two answer choices are really opposites, with just a slight change in the wording shown above. Once you realize these are opposites, you should examine them closely. One of these two is likely to be the correct answer.
Example:
> A.) if other factors are held constant, then increasing the interest rate will lead to a decrease in housing starts
> B.) when there is an increase in housing starts, and other things remaining equal, it is often the result of an increase in interest rates

Make predictions

One convenience of having only a short paragraph to contain information is that you can easily remember the few facts presented, compared to a much longer reading passage full of much more information. As you read and understand the passage and then the question, try to guess what the

- 88 -

answer will be. Remember that four of the five answer choices are wrong, and once you being reading them, your mind will immediately become cluttered with answer choices designed to throw you off. Your mind is typically the most focused immediately after you have read the passage and question and digested its contents. If you can, try to predict what the correct answer will be. You may be surprised at what you can predict.

Quickly scan the choices and see if your prediction is in the listed answer choices. If it is, then you can be quite confident that you have the right answer. It still won't hurt to check the other answer choices, but most of the time, you've got it!

Answer the Question

It may seem obvious to only pick answer choices that answer the question, but COMPASS can create some excellent answer choices that are wrong. Don't pick an answer just because it sounds right, or you believe it to be true. It MUST answer the question. Once you've made your selection, always go back and check it against the question and make sure that you didn't misread the question, and the answer choice does answer the question posed.

Benchmark

One disadvantage of taking a computer based test (if you are taking the computer based version), as opposed to a traditional paper and pencil test, is that you can't make notes directly on the page. More specifically, you can't cross out answers you believe to be wrong as you read through the list of possible answer choices. The computer offers another solution though. After you read the first answer choice, decide if you think it sounds correct or not. If it doesn't, move on to the next answer choice. If it does, click beside the choice to select it. This doesn't mean that you've definitely selected it as your answer choice, it just means that it's the best you've seen thus far. Go ahead and read the next choice. If the next choice is worse than the one you've already selected, keep going to the next answer choice. If the next choice is better than the choice you've already selected, change your selection.

As you read through the list, highlight the choice you think is right. That is your new standard. Every other answer choice must be benchmarked against that standard. That choice is correct until proven otherwise by another answer choice beating it out. Once you've decided that no other answer choice seems as good, do one final check to ensure that it answers the question posed.

New information

Correct answers will usually contain the information listed in the paragraph and question. Rarely will completely new information be inserted into a correct answer choice. Occasionally the new information may be related in a manner than COMPASS is asking for you to interpret, but seldom.

Example:
> The argument above is dependent upon which of the following assumptions?
> A.) Scientists have used Charles's Law to interpret the relationship.

If Charles's Law is not mentioned at all in the referenced paragraph and argument, then it is unlikely that this choice is correct. All of the information needed to answer the question is provided for you, and so you should not have to make guesses that are unsupported or choose answer choices that have unknown information that cannot be reasoned.

Key words

Look for answer choices that have the same key words in them as the question.
Example:
> Which of the following, if true, would best explain the reluctance of politicians since 1980 to support this funding?

Look for the key words "since 1980" to be referenced in the correct answer choice. Most valid answer choices would probably include a phrase such as "since 1980, politicians have..."

Valid information

Don't discount any of the information provided in the passage, particularly shorter ones. Every piece of information may be necessary to determine the correct answer. None of the information in the paragraph is there to throw you off (while the answer choices will certainly have information to throw you off). If two seemingly unrelated topics are discussed, don't ignore either. You can be confident there is a relationship, or it wouldn't be included in the paragraph, and you are probably going to have to determine what is that relationship for the answer.

For additional review help, please check out our COMPASS reading review tutorials, which can be found on the Mometrix Academy: http://www.mometrix.com/academy/compass-reading/

Writing Skills Test

Word confusion

"Which" should be used to refer to things only.

> John's dog, which was called Max, is large and fierce.

"That" may be used to refer to either persons or things.

> Is this the only book that Louis L'Amour wrote?
>
> Is Louis L'Amour the author that [or who] wrote Western novels?

"Who" should be used to refer to persons only.

> Mozart was the composer who [or that] wrote those operas.

Correct pronoun usage in combinations

To determine the correct pronoun form in a compound subject, try each subject separately with the verb, adapting the form as necessary. Your ear will tell you which form is correct.
Example:

> Bob and (I, me) will be going.

Restate the sentence twice, using each subject individually. Bob will be going. I will be going.
> "Me will be going" does not make sense.

When a pronoun is used with a noun immediately following (as in "we boys"), say the sentence without the added noun. Your ear will tell you the correct pronoun form.
Example:

> (We/Us) boys played football last year.

Restate the sentence twice, without the noun. We played football last year. Us played football last year. Clearly "We played football last year" makes more sense.

Punctuation

Punctuation

If a section of text has an opening dash, parentheses, or comma at the beginning of a phrase, then you can be sure there should be a matching closing dash, parentheses, or comma at the end of the phrase. If items in a series all have commas between them, then any additional items in that series will also gain commas. Do not alternate punctuation. If a dash is at the beginning of a statement, then do not put a parenthesis at the ending of the statement.

Commas

Flow

Commas break the flow of text. To test whether they are necessary, while reading the text to yourself, pause for a moment at each comma. If the pauses seem natural, then the commas are correct. If they are not, then the commas are not correct.

Nonessential clauses and phrases

A comma should be used to set off nonessential clauses and nonessential participial phrases from the rest of the sentence. To determine if a clause is essential, remove it from the sentence. If the removal of the clause would alter the meaning of the sentence, then it is essential. Otherwise, it is nonessential.
Example:

John Smith, who was a disciple of Andrew Collins, was a noted archeologist.

In the example above, the sentence describes John Smith's fame in archeology. The fact that he was a disciple of Andrew Collins is not necessary to that meaning. Therefore, separating it from the rest of the sentence with commas, is correct.

Do not use a comma if the clause or phrase is essential to the meaning of the sentence.
Example:

Anyone who appreciates obscure French poetry will enjoy reading the book.

If the phrase "who appreciates obscure French poetry" is removed, the sentence would indicate that anyone would enjoy reading the book, not just those with an appreciation for obscure French poetry. However, the sentence implies that the book's enjoyment may not be for everyone, so the phrase is essential.

Another perhaps easier way to determine if the clause is essential is to see if it has a comma at its beginning or end. Consistent, parallel punctuation must be used, and so if you can determine a comma exists at one side of the clause, then you can be certain that a comma should exist on the opposite side.

Independent clauses

Use a comma before the words and, but, or, nor, for, yet when they join independent clauses. To determine if two clauses are independent, remove the word that joins them. If the two clauses are capable of being their own sentence by themselves, then they are independent and need a comma between them.

Example:

He ran down the street, and then he ran over the bridge.

He ran down the street. Then he ran over the bridge. These are both clauses capable of being their own sentence. Therefore a comma must be used along with the word "and" to join the two clauses together.

If one or more of the clauses would be a fragment if left alone, then it must be joined to another clause and does not need a comma between them.
Example:

He ran down the street and over the bridge.

He ran down the street. Over the bridge. "Over the bridge" is a sentence fragment and is not capable of existing on its own. No comma is necessary to join it with "He ran down the street".

Note that this does not cover the use of "and" when separating items in a series, such as "red, white, and blue". In these cases a comma is not always necessary between the last two items in the series, but in general it is best to use one.

Parenthetical expressions

Commas should separate parenthetical expressions such as the following: after all, by the way, for example, in fact, on the other hand.
Example:

By the way, she is in my biology class.

If the parenthetical expression is in the middle of the sentence, a comma would be both before and after it.
Example:

She is, after all, in my biology class.

However, these expressions are not always used parenthetically. In these cases, commas are not used. To determine if an expression is parenthetical, see if it would need a pause if you were reading the text. If it does, then it is parenthetical and needs commas.
Example:

You can tell by the way she plays the violin that she enjoys its music.

No pause is necessary in reading that example sentence. Therefore the phrase "by the way" does not need commas around it.

Hyphens

Hyphenate a compound adjective that is directly before the noun it describes.

    Example 1: He was the best-known kid in the school.

    Example 2: The shot came from that grass-covered hill.

    Example 3: The well-drained fields were dry soon after the rain.

Semicolons

Period replacement

A semicolon is often described as either a weak period or strong comma. Semicolons should separate independent clauses that could stand alone as separate sentences. To test where a semicolon should go, replace it with a period in your mind. If the two independent clauses would seem normal with the period, then the semicolon is in the right place.

Example:

    The rain had finally stopped; a few rays of sunshine were pushing their way through the clouds.

The rain had finally stopped. A few rays of sunshine were pushing their way through the clouds. These two sentences can exist independently with a period between them. Because they are also closely related in thought, a semicolon is a good choice to combine them.

Transitions

When a semicolon is next to a transition word, such as "however", it comes before the word.

Example:

    The man in the red shirt stood next to her; however, he did not know her name.

If these two clauses were separated with a period, the period would go before the word "however" creating the following two sentences: The man in the red shirt stood next to her. However, he did not know her name. The semicolon can function as a weak period and join the two clauses by replacing the period.

Some questions include a sentence with part or all of it underlined. Your answer choices will offer different ways to reword or rephrase the underlined portion of the sentence.

These questions will test your ability of correct and effective expression. Choose your answer carefully, utilizing the standards of written English, including grammar rules, the proper choice of words and of sentence construction. The correct answer will flow smoothly and be both clear and concise.

Use your ear

Read each sentence carefully, inserting the answer choices in the blanks. Don't stop at the first answer choice if you think it is right, but read them all. What may seem like the best choice, at first, may not be after you have had time to read all of the choices. Allow your ear to determine what sounds right. Often one or two answer choices can be immediately ruled out because it doesn't make sound logical or make sense.

Contextual clues

It bears repeating that contextual clues offer a lot of help in determining the best answer. Key words in the sentence will allow you to determine exactly which answer choice is the best replacement text.
Example:

> Archeology has shown that some of the ruins of the ancient city of Babylon are approximately 500 years <u>as old as any supposed</u> Mesopotamian predecessors.
> A.) as old as their supposed
> B.) older than their supposed

In this example, the key word "supposed" is used. Archaeology would either confirm that the predecessors to Babylon were more ancient or disprove that supposition. Since supposed was used, it would imply that archaeology had disproved the accepted belief, making Babylon actually older, not as old as, and answer choice "B" correct.

Furthermore, because "500 years" is used, answer choice A can be ruled out. Years are used to show either absolute or relative age. If two objects are as old as each other, no years are necessary to describe that relationship, and it would be sufficient to say, "The ancient city of Babylon is approximately as old as their supposed Mesopotamian predecessors," without using the term "500 years".

Simplicity is Bliss

Simplicity cannot be overstated. You should never choose a longer, more complicated, or wordier replacement if a simple one will do. When a point can be made with fewer words, choose that answer. However, never sacrifice the flow of text for simplicity. If an answer is simple, but does not make sense, then it is not correct.

Beware of added phrases that don't add anything of meaning, such as "to be" or "as to them". Often these added phrases will occur just before a colon, which may come before a list of items. However, the colon does not need a lengthy introduction. The italics phrases in the below examples are wordy and unnecessary. They should be removed and the colon placed directly after the words "sport" and "following".
Example 1:

> There are many advantages to running as a sport, *of which the top advantages are*:

Example 2:

 The school supplies necessary were the following, *of which a few are*:

For additional review help, please check out our COMPASS writing review tutorials, which can be found on the Mometrix Academy:

http://www.mometrix.com/academy/compass-writing-skills/

Special Report: COMPASS Secrets in Action

Sample Question: Reading test

Mark Twain was well aware of his celebrity. He was among the first authors to employ a clipping service to track press coverage of himself, and it was not unusual for him to issue his own press statements if he wanted to influence or "spin" coverage of a particular story. The celebrity Twain achieved during his last ten years still reverberates today. Nearly all of his most popular novels were published before 1890, long before his hair grayed or he began to wear his famous white suit in public. We appreciate the author but seem to remember the celebrity.

Based on the passage above, Mark Twain seemed interested in:
   A.   maintaining his celebrity
   B.   selling more of his books
   C.   hiding his private life
   D.   gaining popularity

Let's look at a couple of different methods of solving this problem.

1. Identify the key words in each answer choice.
These are the nouns and verbs that are the most important words in the answer choice.
   A. maintaining, celebrity
   B. selling, books
   C. hiding, life
   D. gaining, popularity

Now try to match up each of the key words with the passage and see where they fit. You're trying to find synonyms and/or exact replication between the key words in the answer choices and key words in the passage.
   A. maintaining – no matches; celebrity – matches in sentences 1, 3, and 5
   B. selling – no matches; books – matches with "novels" in sentence 4.
   C. hiding – no matches; life – no matches
   D. gaining – no matches; popularity –matches with "celebrity" in sentences 1, 3, and 5, because they can be synonyms

At this point there are only two choices that have more than one match, choices A and D, and they both have the same number of matches, and with the same word in the passage, which is the word "celebrity" in the passage. This is a good sign, because COMPASS will often write two answer choices that are close. Having two answer choices pointing towards the same key word is a strong indicator that those key words hold the "key" to finding the right answer.

Now let's compare choice A and D and the unmatched key words. Choice A still has "maintaining" which doesn't have a clear match, while choice D has "gaining" which doesn't have a clear match. While neither of those have clear matches in the passage, ask yourself what are the best arguments that would support any kind of connection with either of those two words.

"Maintaining" makes sense when you consider that Twain was interested in tracking his press coverage and that he was actively managing the "spin" of certain stories.

"Gaining" makes sense when you consider that Twain was actively issuing his own press releases, however one key point to remember is that he was only issuing these press releases after another story was already in existence.

Since Twain's press releases were not being released in a news vacuum, but rather as a response mechanism to ensure control over the angle of a story, his releases were more to *maintain* control over his image, rather than *gain* an image in the first place.

Furthermore, when comparing the terms "popularity" and "celebrity", there are similarities between the words, but in referring back to the passage, it is clear that "celebrity" has a stronger connection to the passage, being the exact word used three times in the passage.

Since "celebrity" has a stronger match than "popularity" and "maintaining" makes more sense than "gaining," it is clear that choice A is correct.

2. Use a process of elimination.
A. maintaining his celebrity – The passage discusses how Mark Twain was both aware of his celebrity status and would take steps to ensure that he got the proper coverage in any news story and maintained the image he desired. This is the correct answer.

B. selling more of his books – Mark Twain's novels are mentioned for their popularity and while common sense would dictate that he would be interested in selling more of his books, the passage makes no mention of him doing anything to promote sales.

C. hiding his private life – While the passage demonstrates that Mark Twain was keenly interested in how the public viewed his life, it does not indicate that he cared about hiding his private life, not even mentioning his life outside of the public eye. The passage deals with how he was seen by the public.

D. gaining popularity – At first, this sounds like a good answer choice, because Mark Twain's popularity is mentioned several times. The main difference though is that he wasn't trying to gain popularity, but simply ensuring that the popularity he had was not distorted by bad press.

Sample Question: Mathematics Test

Three coins are tossed up in the air. What is the probability that two of them will land heads and one will land tails?

  A. 0
  B. 1/8
  C. 1/4
  D. 3/8

Let's look at a few different methods and steps to solving this problem.

1. Reduction and Division

Quickly eliminate the probabilities that you immediately know. You know to roll all heads is a 1/8 probability, and to roll all tails is a 1/8 probability. Since there are in total 8/8 probabilities, you can subtract those two out, leaving you with 8/8 – 1/8 – 1/8 = 6/8. So after eliminating the possibilities of getting all heads or all tails, you're left with 6/8 probability. Because there are only three coins, all other combinations are going to involve one of either head or tail, and two of the other. All other combinations will either be 2 heads and 1 tail, or 2 tails and 1 head. Those remaining combinations both have the same chance of occurring, meaning that you can just cut the remaining 6/8 probability in half, leaving you with a 3/8ths chance that there will be 2 heads and 1 tail, and another 3/8ths chance that there will be 2 tails and 1 head, making choice D correct.

2. Run Through the Possibilities for that Outcome

You know that you have to have two heads and one tail for the three coins. There are only so many combinations, so quickly run through them all.

You could have:
  H, H, H
  H, H, T
  H, T, H
  T, H, H
  T, T, H
  T, H, T
  H, T, T
  T, T, T

Reviewing these choices, you can see that three of the eight have two heads and one tail, making choice D correct.

3. Fill in the Blanks with Symbology and Odds

Many probability problems can be solved by drawing blanks on a piece of scratch paper (or making mental notes) for each object used in the problem, then filling in probabilities and multiplying them out. In this case, since there are three coins being flipped, draw three blanks. In the first blank, put an "H" and over it write "1/2". This represents the case where the first coin is flipped as heads. In that case (where the first coin comes up heads), one of the other two coins must come up tails and one must come up heads to fulfill the criteria posed in the problem (2 heads and 1 tail). In the second blank, put a "1" or "1/1". This is because it doesn't matter what is flipped for the second coin, so long as the first coin is heads. In the third blank, put a "1/2". This is because the third coin must be the exact opposite of whatever is in the second blank. Half the time the third coin will be the same as the second coin, and half the time the third coin will be the opposite, hence the "1/2". Now multiply out the odds. There is a half chance that the first coin will come up "heads", then it doesn't matter for the second coin, then there is a half chance that the third coin will be the opposite of the second coin, which will give the desired result of 2 heads and 1 tail. So, that gives 1/2*1/1*1/2 = 1/4.

But, now you must calculate the probabilities that result if the first coin is flipped tails. So draw another group of three blanks. In the first blank, put a "T" and over it write "1/2". This represents the case where the first coin is flipped as tails. In that case (where the first coin comes up tails), both of the other two coins must come up heads to fulfill the criteria posed in the problem. In the second blank, put an "H" and over it write "1/2". In the third blank, put an "H" and over it write "1/2". Now multiply out the odds. There is a half chance that the first coin will come up "tails", then there is a half chance that the second coin will be heads, and a half chance that the third coin will be heads. So, that gives 1/2*1/2*1/2 = 1/8.

Now, add those two probabilities together. If you flip heads with the first coin, there is a 1/4 chance of ultimately meeting the problem's criteria. If you flip tails with the first coin, there is a 1/8 chance of ultimately meeting the problem's criteria. So, that gives 1/4 + 1/8 = 2/8 + 1/8 = 3/8, which makes choice D correct.

Sample Question: Writing Skills Test

Choose which way of writing the underlined part of the sentence is correct.

<u>As a consumer, one can accept</u> the goods offered to us or we can reject them, but we cannot determine their quality or change the system's priorities.

      A. As a consumer, one can accept

      B. We the consumer either can accept

      C. The consumer can accept

      D. As consumers, we can accept

Let's look at a couple of different methods and steps to solving this problem.

1. Agreement in Pronoun Number

All pronouns have to agree in number to their antecedent or noun that they are representing. In the underlined portion, the pronoun "one" has as its antecedent the noun "consumer".

Go through and match up each of the pronouns in the answer choices with their antecedents.

A. consumer, one – correctly matches singular antecedent to singular pronoun

B. We, consumer – incorrectly matches plural antecedent to singular pronoun

C. consumer – no pronoun

D. consumers, we – correctly matches singular antecedent to singular pronoun

Based on pronoun number agreement, you can eliminate choice B from consideration because it fails the test.

2. Parallelism

Not only do the pronouns and antecedents in the underlined portion of the sentence have to be correct, but the rest of the sentence has to match as well. The remainder of the sentence has to be parallel to the underlined portion. In part of the sentence that is not underlined is the phrase "we can reject them," and another phrase, "but we cannot determine." Notice how both of these phrases use the plural pronoun "we". This means that the underlined portion of the sentence has to agree with the rest of the sentence and have matching plural pronouns and nouns as well.

Quickly review the answer choices and look for whether the nouns and pronouns in the answer choices are singular or plural.

      A. consumer, one – singular noun and singular pronoun

      B. We, consumer – plural pronoun and singular noun

      C. consumer – singular noun

      D. consumers, we – plural noun and plural pronoun

Only choice D has both a plural noun and a plural pronoun, making choice D correct.

Practice Test

Reading Test

Each of the following passages is followed by a series of questions to test the ability to refer to a text to obtain information or to obtain the information through reasoning. Referral questions are derived from material explicitly stated in a passage. Reasoning items test the ability to make appropriate inferences. In each case, select the best choice from the multiple-choice alternatives that follow the text.

Passage 1 – Practical Reading

<u>Cultivation of Tomato Plants</u>

Tomato plants should be started in window boxes or greenhouses in late March so that they will be ready for the garden after the last frost. Use a soil of equal parts of sand, peat moss and manure, and plant the seeds about a quarter of an inch deep. After covering, water them through a cloth to protect the soil and cover the box with a pane of glass. Keep the box in a warm place for a few days, then place it in a sunny window. After the second leaf makes its appearance on the seedling, transplant the plant to another box, placing the seedlings two inches apart. Another alternative is to put the sprouted seedlings in four-inch pots, setting them deeper in the soil than they stood in the seed bed. To make the stem stronger, pinch out the top bud when the seedlings are four or five inches in height.

Finally, place the plants in their permanent positions after they have grown to be twelve or fifteen inches high. When transplanting, parts of some of the longest leaves should be removed. Large plants may be set five or six inches deep.

The soil should be fertilized the previous season. Fresh, stable manure, used as fertilizer, would delay the time of fruiting. To improve the condition of the soil, work in a spade full of old manure to a depth of at least a foot. Nitrate of soda, applied at about two hundred pounds per acre, may be used to give the plant a good start.

Plants grown on supports may be set two feet apart in the row, with the rows three or four feet apart depending upon the variety. Plants not supported by stakes or other methods should be set four feet apart.

Unsupported vines give a lighter yield and much of the fruit is likely to rot during the wet seasons. Use well sharpened stakes about two inches in diameter and five feet long. Drive the stakes into the ground at least six inches from the plants so that the roots will not be injured. Tie the tomato vines to the stakes with strings made out of strips of cloth, as twine is likely to cut them. Care must be taken not to wrap the limbs so tightly as to interfere with their growth. The training should start before the plants begin to trail on the ground.

1. What is the overall purpose of this passage?
    a. To describe how soil should be treated in order to plant tomatoes.
    b. To give an overview of how tomato plants are cultured.
    c. To teach the reader how to operate a farm.
    d. To describe a method of supporting tomato vines.
    e. To explain why plants may wither in cold weather.

2. According to the passage, why is late March the best time to germinate tomato seeds?
    a. The last frost has already passed by this time.
    b. It is warm enough by then to germinate them in window boxes.
    c. By the time the last frost passes, they will be ready to transplant outdoors.
    d. The seeds might not be fertile if one were to wait longer.
    e. They need to be exposed to a frost in order to germinate.

3. What does the passage imply as the reason that the seeds not planted outdoors immediately?
    a. A late freeze might kill the seedlings.
    b. The soil outdoors is too heavy for new seedlings.
    c. A heavy rain might wash away the seedlings.
    d. New seedlings need to be close to one another and then be moved apart later.
    e. The wind might blow the new seedlings down or uproot them.

4. Generally speaking, the culturing method consists of what?
    a. Tying the germinated seedlings to stakes.
    b. Watering the new plants regularly.
    c. Sheltering the plants from wind and frost.
    d. Using scarecrows to keep birds away.
    e. Moving the strongest plants progressively to larger pots and then outdoors.

5. What would happen if the bud weren't pinched out of the seedlings when they are in individual pots?
    a. The plants would be weaker.
    b. The plants would freeze.
    c. The plants would need more water.
    d. The plants would not survive as long.
    e. The plants would not grow as tall.

6. Why are the plants set further apart each time they are replanted?
    a. The soil is being depleted each time they are planted.
    b. The plants are larger and need more soil for nourishment.
    c. More room is required in order to plant the stakes for support.
    d. More room is required so that nitrate of soda can be added.
    e. This makes it more difficult for the birds to find them.

7. Why are the newly planted seeds watered through a cloth?
   a. They are unsightly.
   b. The cloth keeps them warm.
   c. The heavy stream of water may disrupt the soil.
   d. The water needs to be filtered.
   e. The cloth keeps the sun off the seedlings while they are receiving water.

8. What fertilizers mentioned in the text are used optionally to nourish the plants?
   a. Glass pane
   b. Sand
   c. Peat moss
   d. Manure
   e. Nitrate of soda

9. Why is old manure preferred to fresh manure?
   a. Fresh manure delays the plant's production of tomatoes.
   b. Fresh manure smells worse.
   c. Old manure is less expensive.
   d. Old manure mixes more readily with nitrate of soda.
   e. Old manure is flakier and more easily blended with the soil.

10. Why do you suppose supported plants are set farther apart than unsupported ones?
    a. The stakes take up a lot of room.
    b. More room is required to water them.
    c. Unsupported plants grow taller.
    d. The support system lets the vines spread out over a larger area.
    e. Supported plants bear larger fruit.

11. What is the purpose of the last paragraph?
    a. To explain why unsupported plants give rotten fruit.
    b. To explain why cloth is used rather than wire.
    c. To describe in detail how tomato plants are cultured.
    d. To instruct the reader in the method of supporting tomato vines for culture.
    e. To suggest a means of getting larger fruit.

12. When are the plants tied to stakes?
    a. As soon as the plants are transplanted outdoors.
    b. When the plants begin to bear fruit.
    c. Before the plants drag on the ground.
    d. After the last frost once the roots have set.

Passage 2 – Humanities

<u>The Coins of Ancient Greece</u>

We don't usually think of coins as works of art, and most of them really do not invite us to do so. The study of coins, their development and history, is termed *numismatics*. Numismatics is a topic of great interest to archeologists and anthropologists, but not usually from the perspective of visual delectation. The coin is intended, after all, to be a utilitarian object, not an artistic one. Many early Greek coins are aesthetically pleasing as well as utilitarian, however, and not simply because they are the earliest examples of the coin design. Rather, Greek civic individualism provides the reason. Every Greek political entity expressed its identity through its coinage.

The idea of stamping metal pellets of a standard weight with an identifying design had its origin on the Ionian Peninsula around 600 B.C. Each of the Greek city-states produced its own coinage adorned with its particular symbols. The designs were changed frequently to commemorate battles, treaties, and other significant occasions. In addition to their primary use as a pragmatic means of facilitating commerce, Greek coins were clearly an expression of civic pride. The popularity of early coinage led to a constant demand for new designs, such that there arose a class of highly skilled artisans who took great pride in their work, so much so that they sometimes even signed it. As a result, Greek coins provide us not only with an invaluable source of historical knowledge, but also with a genuine expression of the evolving Greek sense of form, as well. These minuscule works reflect the development of Greek sculpture from the sixth to the second century B.C. as dependably as do larger works made of marble or other metals. And since they are stamped with the place and date of their production, they provide an historic record of artistic development that is remarkably dependable and complete.

13. What is the purpose of this passage?
    a. To attract new adherents to numismatics as a pastime.
    b. To show how ancient Greeks used coins in commerce.
    c. To teach the reader that money was invented in Greece.
    d. To describe ancient Greek coinage as an art form
    e. To show why coins are made of precious metals.

14. What is meant by the phrase "most of them do not invite us to do so", as used in the first sentence?
    a. Money is not usually included when sending an invitation.
    b. Most coins are not particularly attractive.
    c. Invitations are not generally engraved onto coins.
    d. Coins do not speak.
    e. It costs money to enter a museum.

15. What is a synonym for "delectation", as used in the third sentence?
    a. Savoring
    b. Choosing
    c. Deciding
    d. Refusing
    e. Consuming

16. What is meant by the term numismatics?
    a. The study of numbers
    b. Egyptian history
    c. Greek history
    d. The study of coins
    e. The study of commerce

17. According to the text, how do ancient Greek coins differ from most other coinage?
    a. Simply because they were the first coins.
    b. Each political entity made its own coins.
    c. They were made of precious metals.
    d. They had utilitarian uses.
    e. They were designed with extraordinary care.

18. How often were new coins designed in ancient Greece?
    a. Monthly
    b. Not very often.
    c. Whenever there was a significant occasion to commemorate.
    d. When the old ones wore out.
    e. In the year 600 B.C.

19. What is indicated by the fact that the artisans who designed the coins sometimes signed them?
    a. They took pride in their work.
    b. They were being held accountable for their work.
    c. The signature certified the value of the coin.
    d. The Greeks had developed writing.
    e. The coins that were signed were the most valuable.

20. What is meant by the term *pragmatic*, as used in the third sentence of the second paragraph?
    a. Valuable
    b. Monetary
    c. Useful
    d. Officious
    e. Practical

21. According to the passage, how are Greek coins similar to Greek sculpture?
    a. Some sculptures were made of metal.
    b. The coins were smaller.
    c. Shapes were stamped into the coins.
    d. Coin designs evolved along with the Greek sense of form.
    e. Both had pragmatic applications.

22. Why is it significant that new coin designs were required frequently?
    a. This indicates that there was a lot of commercial activity going on.
    b. This gave the designers a lot of practice.
    c. There were a lot of things to commemorate.
    d. The Greeks needed to find new sources of precious metals.
    e. The older coins could be recycled.

23. Why is it significant that the coins were dated, according to the passage?
    a. The dates contributed to the designs
    b. The age of the designers could be determined.
    c. It allows historians to track the evolution of Greek artistic styles.
    d. It allows historians to know when battles and treaties took place.
    e. It allows historians to know when the artisans who signed the coins lived.

24. What was the primary purpose of the Greek coin?
    a. To commemorate treaties and battles.
    b. To provide minuscule works of art.
    c. They were used as adornments.
    d. To facilitate commerce.
    e. To provide an invaluable source of historical knowledge.

Passage 3 – Prose Fiction

Garth

The next morning she realized that she had slept. This surprised her – so long had sleep been denied her! She opened her eyes and saw the sun at the window. And then, beside it in the window, the deformed visage of Garth. Quickly, she shut her eyes again, feigning sleep. But he was not fooled. Presently she heard his voice, soft and kind: "Don't be afraid. I'm your friend. I came to watch you sleep, is all. There now, I am behind the wall. You can open your eyes."

The voice seemed pained and plaintive. The Hungarian opened her eyes, saw the window empty. Steeling herself, she arose, went to it, and looked out. She saw the man below, cowering by the wall, looking grief-stricken and resigned. Making an effort to overcome her revulsion, she spoke to him as kindly as she could.

"Come," she said, but Garth, seeing her lips move, thought she was sending him away. He rose and began to lumber off, his eyes lowered and filled with despair.

"Come!" she cried again, but he continued to move off. Then, she swept from the cell, ran to him and took his arm. Feeling her touch, Garth trembled uncontrollably. Feeling that she drew him toward her, he lifted his supplicating eye and his whole face lit up with joy.

She drew him into the garden, where she sat upon a wall, and for a while they sat and contemplated one another. The more the Hungarian looked at Garth, the more deformities she discovered. The twisted spine, the lone eye, the huge torso over the tiny legs. She couldn't comprehend how a creature so awkwardly constructed could exist. And yet, from the air of sadness and gentleness that pervaded his figure, she began to reconcile herself to it.

"Did you call me back?" asked he.

"Yes," she replied, nodding. He recognized the gesture.

"Ah," he exclaimed. "Do you know that I am deaf?"

"Poor fellow," exclaimed the Hungarian, with an expression of pity.

"You'd think nothing more could be wrong with me," Garth put in, somewhat bitterly. But he was happier than he could remember having been.

25.   Why was the girl surprised that she had slept?
   a.   It was afternoon.
   b.   She seldom slept.
   c.   It had been a long time since she had had the chance to sleep.
   d.   She hadn't intended to go to sleep.
   e.   Garth looked so frightening that she thought he would keep her awake.

26.   Why did she shut her eyes again when she saw Garth in the window?
   a.   She wanted to sleep some more.
   b.   The sun was so bright that it hurt her eyes.
   c.   She didn't want to look at Garth.
   d.   She wanted Garth to think she was still sleeping.
   e.   She was trying to remember how she got there.

27.   What two characteristics are contrasted in Garth?
     a.   Ugliness and gentleness
     b.   Fear and merriment
     c.   Distress and madness
     d.   Happiness and sadness
     e.   Anger and fearfulness

28.   During this passage, how do the girl's emotions toward Garth change?
     a.   They go from fear to loathing.
     b.   They go from anger to fear.
     c.   They go from hatred to disdain.
     d.   They go from fear to disdain.
     e.   They go from revulsion to pity.

29.   Why does the girl have to steel herself to approach the window and look out at Garth?
     a.   She is groggy from sleep.
     b.   She has not eaten for a long time.
     c.   She is repelled by his appearance.
     d.   She is blinded by the sun behind him.
     e.   The window is open and it is cold.

30.   How does Garth feel toward the girl when he first moves away from the window?
     a.   He is curious about her.
     b.   He is sad because she appears to reject him.
     c.   He is angry at her for pretending to sleep.
     d.   He pretends to be indifferent toward her.
     e.   He expects her to scold him.

31.   Why does Garth withdraw from the girl when she first speaks to him?
     a.   He expects her to hurt him.
     b.   He misunderstands her because he cannot hear.
     c.   People are always mean to him.
     d.   He thinks she wants to sleep some more.
     e.   He doesn't want her to feel revulsion because of his appearance.

32.   What is a synonym for the word *supplicating*?
     a.   Castigating
     b.   Menacing
     c.   Repeating
     d.   Begging
     e.   Steeling

33.   Why is it surprising that the girl takes Garth's arm?
   a.   She is engaged to someone else.
   b.   She has to reach through the window.
   c.   He is deaf.
   d.   She was very frightened of him initially.
   e.   His clothes are dirty.

34.   Which of the following adjectives might you use to describe the girl's personality?
   a.   Determined
   b.   Robust
   c.   Manic
   d.   Contemplative
   e.   Sympathetic

35.   Which of the following adjectives would you use to describe Garth's feelings toward himself?
   a.   Contemplative
   b.   Destitute
   c.   Unhappy
   d.   Deflated
   e.   Jaunty

36.   Why is Garth so happy in the last sentence?
   a.   Because he can understand the girl.
   b.   He has learned to read lips.
   c.   Because the girl figured out that he is deaf.
   d.   Because the girl seems to accept him.
   e.   Because the sun is shining.

Passage 4 – Social Sciences

New Zealand Inhabitants

The islands of New Zealand are among the most remote of all the Pacific islands. New Zealand is an archipelago, with two large islands and a number of smaller ones. Its climate is far cooler than the rest of Polynesia. Nevertheless, according to Maori legends, it was colonized in the early fifteenth century by a wave of Polynesian voyagers who traveled southward in their canoes and settled on North Island. At this time, New Zealand was already known to the Polynesians, who had probably first landed there some 400 years earlier.

The Polynesian southward migration was limited by the availability of food. Traditional Polynesian tropical crops such as taro and yams will grow on North

- 111 -

Island, but the climate of South Island is too cold for them. Coconuts will not grow on either island. The first settlers were forced to rely on hunting and gathering, and, of course, fishing. Especially on South Island, most settlements remained close to the sea. At the time of the Polynesian influx, enormous flocks of moa birds had their rookeries on the island shores. These flightless birds were easy prey for the settlers, and within a few centuries had been hunted to extinction. Fish, shellfish and the roots of the fern were other important sources of food, but even these began to diminish in quantity as the human population increased. The Maori had few other sources of meat: dogs, smaller birds, and rats. Archaeological evidence shows that human flesh was also eaten, and that tribal warfare increased markedly after the moa disappeared.

By far the most important farmed crop in prehistoric New Zealand was the sweet potato. This tuber is hearty enough to grow throughout the islands, and could be stored to provide food during the winter months, when other food-gathering activities were difficult. The availability of the sweet potato made possible a significant increase in the human population. Maori tribes often lived in encampments called *pa*, which were fortified with earthen embankments and usually located near the best sweet potato farmlands.

37. A definition for the word *archipelago* is
   a. A country
   b. A place in the southern hemisphere
   c. A group of islands
   d. A roosting place for birds
   e. A place with rainforests

38. This article is primarily about what?
   a. The geology of New Zealand
   b. New Zealand's early history
   c. New Zealand's prehistory
   d. Food sources used by New Zealand's first colonists.
   e. Polynesian emigration.

39. According to the passage, when was New Zealand first settled?
   a. In the fifteenth century
   b. Around the eleventh century
   c. Thousands of years ago
   d. By flightless birds
   e. On South Island

40. Why did early settlements remain close to the sea?
    a. The people liked to swim.
    b. The people didn't want to get far from the boats they had come in.
    c. Taro and yams grow only close to the beaches.
    d. The seaside climate was milder.
    e. They were dependent upon sea creatures for their food.

41. Why do you suppose tribal warfare increased after the moa disappeared?
    a. Increased competition for food led the people to fight.
    b. Some groups blamed others for the moa's extinction.
    c. They had more time on their hands since they couldn't hunt the moa, so they fought.
    d. One group was trying to consolidate political control over the entire country.
    e. They wanted to appease the gods in the hope that the moa would return.

42. How did the colder weather of New Zealand make it difficult for the Polynesians to live there?
    a. The Polynesians weren't used to making warm clothes.
    b. Cold water fish are harder to catch.
    c. Some of them froze.
    d. Some of their traditional crops would not grow there.
    e. They had never seen snow.

43. What was a significant difference between the sweet potato and other crops known to the Polynesians?
    a. The sweet potato provided more protein.
    b. The sweet potato would grow on North Island.
    c. The sweet potato could be stored during the winter.
    d. The sweet potato could be cultured near their encampments.
    e. The sweet potato did not need to be cultured near the shores.

44. Why was it important that sweet potatoes could be stored?
    a. They could be eaten in winter, when other foods were scarce.
    b. They could be traded for fish and other goods.
    c. They could be taken along by groups of warriors going to war.
    d. They tasted better after a few weeks of storage.
    e. They were kept in pa.

45. Why do you suppose the *pa* were usually located near sweet potato farmlands?
    a. So they could defend the best farmlands from their fortified camps.
    b. So they could have ready access to their most important source of food.
    c. So they could transport the potatoes easily into camp for storage.
    d. So they wouldn't have far to go from camp to work in the farmlands.
    e. All of the above are probably true.

46. Why might the shellfish populations have diminished as the human population increased?
    a. Too many people poisoned the waters.
    b. The shellfish didn't like people and migrated elsewhere.
    c. The people were hunting the natural predators of the shellfish to extinction.
    d. There were fewer nutrients left in the waters for the shellfish.
    e. The humans were eating the shellfish faster than they could replenish themselves through reproduction.

47. What was it about the moa that made them easy for the Maori to catch?
    a. They were fat.
    b. They roosted by the shore.
    c. They were not very smart.
    d. They were brightly colored.
    e. They were unable to fly.

48. What might have been one of the reasons that the Maori practiced cannibalism?
    a. They were starving so they turned to human flesh.
    b. The Polynesians had a tradition of cannibalism, which they brought with them to New Zealand.
    c. Human flesh tasted a lot like moa.
    d. They were fighting over the sweet potato farmlands.
    e. They didn't know how to bury their dead.

Passage 5 – Natural Sciences

Annelids

The phylum Annelida, named for the Latin word *anellus*, meaning "ring", includes earthworms, leeches, and other similar organisms. In their typical form, these animals exhibit bilateral symmetry, a cylindrical cross section, and an elongate body divided externally into segments (*metameres*) by a series of rings (*annuli*). They are segmented internally as well, with most of the internal organs repeated in series in each segment. This organization is termed *metamerism*. Metameric segmentation is the distinguishing feature of this phylum, and provides it with a degree of evolutionary plasticity in that certain segments can be modified and specialized to perform specific functions. For example, in some species certain of the locomotor *parapodia*, or feet, may be modified for grasping, and some portions of the gut may evolve digestive specializations.

The gut is a straight, muscular tube that functions independently of the muscular activity in the body wall. The Annelida resemble the nematodes, another worm phylum, in possessing a fluid-filled internal cavity separating the gut from the body wall. In both phyla, this cavity is involved in locomotion. However, in the annelids

- 114 -

this space is formed at a much later time during the development of the embryo, and presumably evolved much later as well. This fluid-filled internal space is called a true *coelum*.

The annelid excretory and circulatory systems are well developed, and some members of the phylum have evolved respiratory organs. The nervous system offers a particular example of metameric specialization. It is concentrated anteriorly into enlarged cerebral ganglia connected to a ventral nerve cord that extends posteriorly and is organized into repeating segmental ganglia.

This phylum includes members bearing adaptations required for aquatic (marine or freshwater) or terrestrial habitats. They may be free-living entities or exist as parasites. Among the best known are the earthworm *Lumbricus*, the water leech *Hirudo*, and the marine worm *Nereis*.

49. What is the purpose of this passage?
   a. To describe the annelid nervous system.
   b. To describe the annelid digestive system.
   c. To introduce distinctive features of annelid anatomy.
   d. To define metamerism.
   e. To tell readers about earthworms.

50. What is meant by the term *metamerism*?
   a. Segmentation of the anatomy
   b. A series of rings
   c. Bilateral symmetry
   d. Evolutionary plasticity
   e. Specialization

51. What is meant by the term *parapodia*?
   a. Specialization
   b. Grasping appendages
   c. Locomotion
   d. Metameres
   e. Feet

52. One evolutionary advantage of segmentation is that
   a. Segmented animals have many feet.
   b. Segmented animals have a fluid-filled coelum.
   c. Parts of some segments can become specialized to perform certain functions.
   d. Segments can evolve.
   e. Segments are separated by rings.

53.	A group of worms other than the Annelida are called
   a.	Lumbricus
   b.	Nematodes
   c.	Leeches
   d.	Parapodia
   e.	Metameres

54.	Some annelid feet may be specialized in order to
   a.	be used for locomotion.
   b.	be segmented.
   c.	be fluid-filled.
   d.	evolve.
   e.	grasp things.

55.	A difference between the annelid coelum and the fluid-filled cavity of other worms is that
   a.	the annelid coelum is involved in locomotion.
   b.	the annelid coelum is formed later.
   c.	the annelid coelum is formed during embryology.
   d.	the annelid coelum is cylindrical in cross section.
   e.	the annelid coelum separates the gut from the body wall.

56.	An example of metameric specialization in the nervous system is
   a.	segmental ganglia.
   b.	the ventral nerve cord.
   c.	respiratory organs.
   d.	parpapodia
   e.	cerebral ganglia

57.	The main difference between the Annelida and all other animal phyla is that
   a.	the Annelida are worms.
   b.	the Annelida include the leeches.
   c.	the Annelida are metameric.
   d.	the Annelida are aquatic.
   e.	the Annelida are specialized.

58.	The purpose of the last paragraph in the passage is to
   a.	give familiar examples of members of the annelid phylum.
   b.	show that annelids may be parasites.
   c.	tell the reader that annelids may be adapted to aquatic environments.
   d.	show that there are many annelids in nature and that they are adapted to a wide variety of habitats.
   e.	tell the reader that earthworms are annelids.

59.   The fluid-filled cavity in the nematodes is used for
    a.   defense.
    b.   reproduction.
    c.   feeding.
    d.   the gut.
    e.   movement.

60.   Members of the Annelida are
    a.   free-living animals.
    b.   parasites.
    c.   aquatic.
    d.   terrestrial.
    e.   all the above

Math Test

For each question, select the choice which provides the best answer.

Numerical Skills / Prealgebra

1. $18 + 7 - (-5) + 11 = ?$
    a. 31
    b. 41
    c. 51
    d. 21
    e. 11

2. Luis left home with $5.50 in his wallet. He spent $3.25 on drinks and $2.00 on a magazine. Later, his friend repaid him $3.50 that he had borrowed the previous day. How much did Luis have in his wallet then?
    a. $12.25
    b. $14.25
    c. $3.25
    d. $3.75
    e. $1.75

3. $\frac{1}{3} + \left(\frac{1}{5} \times \frac{2}{3}\right) - \left(\frac{2}{5} \times \frac{1}{3}\right) = ?$
    a. $\frac{1}{3}$
    b. $-\frac{1}{3}$
    c. $\frac{2}{15}$
    d. $-\frac{2}{15}$
    e. $\frac{3}{15}$

4. John needed 13.71 feet of wire to fix a lamp. He bought $14\frac{1}{2}$ feet of wire at the hardware store. How much wire did he have left over after fixing the lamp?
    a. $\frac{3}{4}$ ft
    b. 0.29 ft
    c. 0.81 ft
    d. 1.29 ft
    e. 0.79 ft

5. A music club offers 7 CDs for $24 to new members. The usual price of CDs is $12 each. If Maria joins the club and gets her 7 CDs at the discounted price instead of buying them individually, how much is her total savings?

    a. $53

    b. $24

    c. $84

    d. $60

    e. $79

6. $7,600,000 - 24,000 = ?$

    a. 7.576×10^6

    b. 7.36×10^6

    c. 7.84×10^6

    d. 7.576×10^5

    e. 7.84×10^5

7. Which of the following expressions is equivalent to $3 < x^{\frac{1}{2}} < 5$?

    a. $3 < x < 5$

    b. $3 < x < 15$

    c. $9 < x < 15$

    d. $9 < x < 25$

    e. $3 < x < 25$

8. $3 \times \sqrt[3]{27} = ?$

    a. 3

    b. 81

    c. 27

    d. 9

    e. 8

9. What is the value of x if $\frac{7}{11} = \frac{x}{7}$?

    a. 7

    b. $\frac{49}{11}$

    c. 77

    d. 121

    e. $\frac{11}{7}$

10. If 12 gallons of gasoline costs $48.75, what is the cost of 13 gallons of gasoline?
   a. $50.25
   b. $\frac{12}{13} \times \$48.75$
   c. $\frac{13}{12} \times \$48.75$
   d. $\frac{\$48.75}{12 \times 13}$
   e. $\frac{12 \times 13}{\$48.75}$

11. Fifty-five people take a math exam. Eighty percent of them pass. How many people failed the exam?
   a. 5.5
   b. 10
   c. 16
   d. 44
   e. 11

12. Three quarters of the participants in a bicycle race crossed the finish line in less than 3 hours. How many finished in less than 3 hours?
   a. 25%
   b. $\frac{3}{4}\%$
   c. 75%
   d. 67%
   e. 50%

13. Ricky took the SAT math test four times. The first three scores totaled 1900. After fourth time, his average score was 650. What score did he get the fourth time?
   a. 600
   b. 650
   c. 700
   d. 750
   e. 800

14. Three quarters of the students running a 100-yard race finished with an average time of 16 seconds. The remaining 25% of students finished with an average time of 12 seconds. What was the average time overall?
   a. 13 seconds
   b. 14 seconds
   c. 15 seconds
   d. 16 seconds
   e. 17 seconds

15. Manuella makes $21 in commissions over the first three hours that she worked selling magazines. How many dollars must she make during the fourth hour to average $8 an hour for the full four hours?

    a. $8

    b. $11

    c. $12

    d. $15

    e. $10

Algebra

16. Let $= \frac{x^4-2}{x^2+1}$. If x = -2, what is the value of y?

    a. $-3\frac{3}{5}$

    b. $2\frac{4}{5}$

    c. $-2\frac{4}{5}$

    d. $2\frac{2}{3}$

    e. $2\frac{4}{9}$

17. To determine if a person is overweight, doctors often calculate a Body Mass Index, or BMI. The BMI is determined by the equation $BMI = \frac{4.88 \times weight}{height^2}$ where the weight is in pounds and the height in feet. What is the approximate BMI for a 110 lb person who is 5 feet tall?

    a. 35.4

    b. 21.5

    c. 16.5

    d. 28.2

    e. 25.2

18. The time t required to fill a cylindrical water tank of radius r and height h is determined to be twice the product of the height and the square of the radius divided by the flow rate V. Which of the following expressions can be used to calculate t?

    a. $\frac{1}{2}Vhr^2$

    b. $\frac{hr^2}{2V}$

    c. $\frac{Vh^2}{2r}$

    d. $\frac{2hr^2}{V}$

    e. $\frac{2r^2}{hV}$

19. A ski club charges a $48 membership fee, plus $18 to rent ski equipment per day. Which of the following equations can be used to find the total cost of membership at the club, when renting equipment for x days?

    a. $y = 66x$
    b. $y = 18x - 48$
    c. $y = 48x + 18$
    d. $y = 54x$
    e. $y = 18x + 48$

20. Which of the following is equivalent to the expression $3x + 5y - (2y - 7x)$?

    a. $-4x + 3y$
    b. $-4x - 7y$
    c. $4x + 3y$
    d. $10x - 3y$
    e. $10x + 3y$

21. Which of the following is the sum of the polynomials $5x^2 - 4x + 1$ and $-3x^2 + x - 3$?

    a. $8x^2 - 5x - 2$
    b. $2x^2 + 3x + 2$
    c. $2x^2 - 3x - 2$
    d. $-8x^2 - 3x - 2$
    e. $-2x^2 - 3x - 2$

22. Which of the following expressions is a factor of the polynomial $x^2 - 4x - 21$?

    a. $(x - 4)$
    b. $(x - 3)$
    c. $(x + 7)$
    d. $(x - 7)$
    e. $(x + 4)$

23. Which of the following is equivalent to $27x^3 + y^3$?

    a. $(3x + y)(3x + y)(3x + y)$
    b. $(3x + y)(9x^2 - 3xy + y^2)$
    c. $(3x - y)(9x^2 + 3xy + y^2)$
    d. $(3x - y)(9x^2 + 9xy + y^2)$
    e. $(3x - y)(3x + y)3xy$

24. To convert temperatures from degrees Celsius (C) to degrees Fahrenheit (F), one can use the equation $= \frac{9C}{5} + 32$. What is the Fahrenheit equivalent of the temperature 18 degrees Celsius?

    a. 64.4
    b. 32.4
    c. 42
    d. 90
    e. 84.4

25. If $\frac{1}{2}x + 2 = 0.75x$, then x = ?

    a. 0.75
    b. 0.5
    c. 2
    d. 4
    e. 8

26. For all nonzero values of q, r, and s, the expression $-\frac{12q^3r^4s^3}{3r^2s^4}$ is equivalent to:

    a. $4\frac{qr^2s}{s^2}$
    b. $-4qrs$
    c. $-4\frac{q^3r^2}{s}$
    d. $4qrs$
    e. $4\frac{q^3r^2}{s}$

27. For all $x > 0$ and $y \neq 0$, which of the following expressions is equivalent to $\sqrt{\frac{x^4}{y^5}}$?

    a. $\frac{x^2\sqrt{y}}{y^2}$
    b. $\frac{x^2\sqrt{y}}{y^3}$
    c. $\frac{x^2}{y^3}$
    d. $\frac{x^2}{y^2\sqrt{y}}$
    e. $x^2\sqrt{y}$

28. Which of the following is an expression equivalent to $\dfrac{a^8 b^{-9} c^2}{a^{-3} b^6 c^4}$?

    a. $\dfrac{a^5 c^2}{b^3}$

    b. $\dfrac{a^5}{b^3 c^2}$

    c. $\dfrac{a^5}{b^{15} c^2}$

    d. $\dfrac{a^{11}}{b^3 c^2}$

    e. $\dfrac{a^{11}}{b^{15} c^2}$

29. What is the slope of the line described by the equation $= 17x - 4$?

    a. 17

    b. -17

    c. 4

    d. -4

    e. $-\dfrac{17}{4}$

30. What is the value of the y-intercept of the line described by the equation $2x + 3y - 7 = 0$?

    a. 7

    b. -7

    c. $\dfrac{7}{3}$

    d. $-\dfrac{7}{3}$

    e. 2

College Algebra

31. What is the next term in the geometric sequence 2, -4, 8, -16?

    a. 8

    b. -8

    c. 32

    d. -32

    e. 24

32. Simple interest I is calculated with the formula $I = Prt$ where P is the principal amount (in dollars), r is the annual interest rate, and t is the time in years. How much interest will be paid on a $15,000 investment at 3% for two years?

    a. $900

    b. $450

    c. $5,000

    d. $300

    e. $4,500

33. Let $f(x) = 2x + 1$ and $(x) = \frac{1}{3}x$. If $x = 4$, what is the value of g(f(x))?

   a. 7

   b. 4

   c. 3

   d. 2

   e. 1

34. Which of the following expressions is equivalent to $\sqrt[3]{8x^5y^7}$?

   a. A. $8^3x^{15}y^{21}$

   b. B. $8^3x^{\frac{5}{3}}y^{\frac{21}{3}}$

   c. C. $2x^{15}y^{21}$

   d. D. $2x^{\frac{5}{3}}y^{\frac{7}{3}}$

   e. E. $2(xy)^3$

35. If $A = \begin{bmatrix} 1 & -3 \\ -4 & 2 \end{bmatrix}$ and $B = \begin{bmatrix} 1 & -3 \\ -4 & -2 \end{bmatrix}$, then $A - B\ = ?$

   a. $\begin{bmatrix} 2 & -6 \\ -8 & 0 \end{bmatrix}$

   b. $\begin{bmatrix} 0 & 0 \\ 0 & 0 \end{bmatrix}$

   c. $\begin{bmatrix} 0 & 0 \\ 0 & 4 \end{bmatrix}$

   d. $\begin{bmatrix} 0 & 3 \\ 4 & 2 \end{bmatrix}$

   e. $\begin{bmatrix} 0 & -6 \\ -8 & 0 \end{bmatrix}$

36. If $f(x) = x^2 + 9x + 21$ and $g(x) = 2(x + 5)^2$, which of the following is an equivalent form of $f(x) - g(x)$?

   a. $-x^2 - 11x - 29$

   b. $x^2 + 11x + 29$

   c. $x + 4$

   d. $x^2 + 7x + 11$

   e. $-(x + 4)$

37. What is the value of $f(g(6))$ if $f(x) = 2x + 6$ and $(x) = x^2 + 5$?

   a. 40

   b. 45

   c. 88

   d. 263

   e. 38

38. The expression $-2i \times 7i$ is equal to
    a. -14
    b. 14
    c. $14\sqrt{-1}$
    d. $-14\sqrt{-1}$
    e. $14\sqrt{i}$

39. If y varies inversely with x, and $y = -6$ when $x = 14$, what is the value of x when $y = -11$?
    a. $\dfrac{6}{14}$
    b. $-\dfrac{6}{14}$
    c. $-7\dfrac{7}{11}$
    d. $7\dfrac{6}{14}$
    e. $7\dfrac{7}{11}$

40. $[0.2 \quad 3.2 \quad -4.1] - [2 \quad 1.7 \quad 1.9] = ?$
    a. $[-1.8 \quad 1.5 \quad -2.2]$
    b. $[-2.2 \quad 4.9 \quad 2.2]$
    c. $-[-2.2 \quad 1.8 \quad 2.2]$
    d. $[-1.8 \quad 1.5 \quad -6.0]$
    e. $[-2.2 \quad 1.5 \quad 2.2]$

Geometry

41. A painter uses 1 quart of paint for every 10 square feet of wall that he paints. He must paint a rectangular wall 12 feet high by 17 feet long, in which there are two circular windows, each one 4 feet in diameter. Which of the following is the closest estimate of the number of quarts of paint he needs?
    a. 24
    b. 12
    c. 120
    d. 180
    e. 18

42. Line $\overline{DE}$ bisects the angle $\angle ACB$ in the isosceles triangle shown in the Figure, in which side $\overline{AC}$ = side $\overline{BC}$. If $\angle DAC$ = 50 degrees, what is $\angle ACE$?

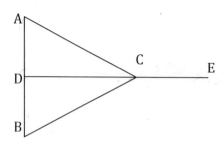

a. 100 degrees
b. 120 degrees
c. 140 degrees
d. 160 degrees
e. 180 degrees

43. A model railroad track is placed on a square board. The track is circular, and is the largest possible track that can fit onto the board so that it reaches the edges of the board on all four sides. What is the length of the track if the length of the side of the square is a?

   a. $2\pi a$
   b. $\dfrac{\pi a}{2}$
   c. $\pi\dfrac{a^2}{2}$
   d. πa^2
   e. πa

44. In the Figure shown here, $\triangle ABC$ is a right triangle. What is the length of side $\overline{AB}$ if side $\overline{BC}$ = 12 ft and side $\overline{AC}$ = 13 ft?

   a. 11 ft
   b. 5 ft
   c. 7 ft
   d. 14 ft
   e. 3 ft

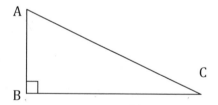

45. In the Figure shown here, the arc $\widehat{AB}$ is 4 meters long, and the total perimeter of the circle is 48 meters. Which of the following best represents the measure of $\angle AOB$, which subtends arc $\widehat{AB}$?

   a. 15 degrees
   b. 30 degrees
   c. 45 degrees
   d. 60 degrees
   e. 75 degrees

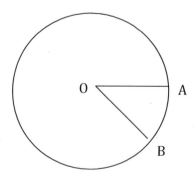

46. A manufacturer uses an aluminum can 4 inches in diameter and 8 inches tall to sell soup. The manufacturer wants to switch to a cylindrical glass jar with a base only 3 inches in diameter. Which of the following best represents the required height of the glass jar, if the jar is to hold exactly the same amount of soup?

a. $12\frac{4}{9}$ inches

b. $10\frac{1}{4}$ inches

c. $11\frac{2}{9}$ inches

d. $9\frac{4}{9}$ inches

e. $14\frac{1}{4}$ inches

47. A circle has a center at the origin. A line tangent to the circle touches the circle at the point, (−5, 6). Which of the following represents the equation of the tangent line?

a. $y - 6 = \frac{5}{6}(x + 5)$

b. $y - 5 = \frac{5}{6}(x + 6)$

c. $y - 6 = -\frac{6}{5}(x + 5)$

d. $y + 5 = \frac{6}{5}(x - 6)$

e. $y + 6 = -\frac{5}{6}(x + 5)$

48. In the Figure shown here, the height of the right trapezoid ABCD is 3 units and the other dimensions are as shown. What is the total area of the trapezoid?

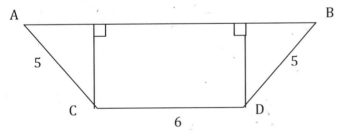

a. 36

b. 24

c. 30

d. 26 ½

49. In the Figure shown here, point E is equidistant between C and D, and ABCD is a square with side equal to a. What is the area of the triangle $\triangle BAE$?

a. $\dfrac{a^2}{2}$

b. $\dfrac{a^2}{4}$

c. $\dfrac{2a^2}{3}$

d. $\dfrac{3a^2}{4}$

e. $\dfrac{a^2}{8}$

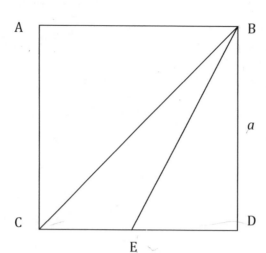

50. In the Figure shown here, not drawn to scale, two circles are shown. The larger circle has area A and radius R. The smaller circle has area a and radius r. If $\dfrac{a}{A} = \dfrac{1}{4}$, then which of the following is true?

a. $\dfrac{r}{R} = \dfrac{1}{2}$

b. $\dfrac{r}{R} = \dfrac{1}{4}$

c. $\dfrac{r}{R} = \dfrac{1}{8}$

d. $\dfrac{R}{r} = \dfrac{1}{4}$

e. $\dfrac{R}{r} = \dfrac{1}{2}$

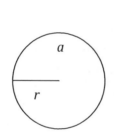
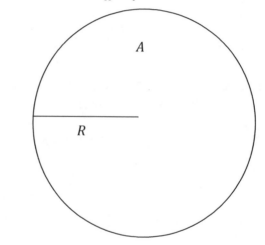

51. A sector is formed within a circle, with a radius of 4 cm and a central angle measure of 145°. Which of the following best represents the area of the sector?

    a. 16.8 cm^2

    b. 18.2 cm^2

    c. 24.8 cm^2

    d. 20.2 cm^2

    e. 26.4 cm^2

Trigonometry

52. The reciprocal of the cosine is called the
    a. sine
    b. secant
    c. cosecant
    d. tangent
    e. cotangent

53. If $\cos A = \frac{2}{5}$, then $\tan A =$
    a. $\frac{5}{2}$
    b. $\sqrt{21}$
    c. $2\sqrt{21}$
    d. $\frac{\sqrt{21}}{2}$
    e. $\frac{2\sqrt{21}}{2}$

54. In the Figure shown here, angle $\angle ACB$ equals 30 degrees, and side $\overline{AC}$ = 13 units. Which of the following best represents the length of side $\overline{BC}$?
    a. 5.2
    b. 11.3
    c. 15.4
    d. 10.3
    e. 8.5

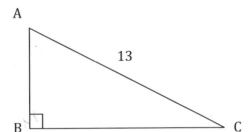

55. Referring again to the Figure above, what is the angle $\angle BAC$?
    a. 45°
    b. 30°
    c. 70°
    d. 60°
    e. 90°

56. A sailor observing a distant lighthouse measures the angle between the base and the top of the lighthouse as 5°. He knows that the lighthouse is 350 feet tall. What is the approximate distance from the sailor to the top of the lighthouse, in feet?

    a. 3000

    b. 4000

    c. 5000

    d. 10,000

    e. 1000

Lighthouse

5°

57. What is the minimum possible range value of the function $\cos \theta$?

    a. 1

    b. 0

    c. -1

    d. $-\infty$

    e. -2π

58. Which of the following measurements in radians is equivalent to 45°?

    a. 2π

    b. π

    c. $\dfrac{\pi}{2}$

    d. $\dfrac{\pi}{4}$

    e. $\dfrac{\pi}{8}$

59. What is the maximum value of the function $f(\theta) = 6 \sin \theta$, for $-2\pi < \theta < 2\pi$?

    a. 6

    b. 6θ

    c. 1

    d. ∞

    e. 12

60. If $\sin \alpha = \dfrac{5}{18}$ and $\cos \alpha = \dfrac{1}{3}$, then $\tan \alpha = ?$

    a. 6

    b. $\dfrac{3}{5}$

    c. $\dfrac{1}{18}$

    d. 3

    e. $\dfrac{5}{6}$

Writing Test

The passages below contain several underlined sections, each of which may or may not contain an error of grammar, usage, or style. For each multiple-choice question, the first choice reproduces the selection from the original passage. The other choices offer alternatives. Select the best choice from among the five choices offered for each underlined selection.

Passage 1– Dyes

(1)People have always color fabrics with dyes. (2)People use to get dyes (3)from those plants they found around them. Different regions had different plants (4)and variously techniques for dyeing. In colonial days, (5)dyeing in Europe were craft skills (6)gained by lengthy apprenticeship. The men who practiced these arts knew biology and chemistry to understand their (7)materials which came from plants, minerals, and animals. (8)Manufacturing natural dyes required much skill, especially for complicated dyes like indigo.

(9)Indigo is maybe the oldest natural dye. The indigo plant stands three feet tall and (10)the dye comprises only 1/2% of the plant's weight. (11)Lots of species of three different plant families, widely scattered over the world, contain enough dye to be worth cultivating, (12)but tropical were especially prized for the quality of color they produced. (13)From India and Africa, for example, came the best indigo.

(14)Native Americans were for long expert dyers before the arrival of Europeans. The American colonists (15)used their dyes and methods they brought from Europe, (16)but over time they turned to dyes made from native plants, as well, (17)to supplant those imported from Europe. During the early 19th century, (18)dyeing becomes a specialized skill and (19)sometimes moved outside the home to a special site. While most women continued to dye many fabrics at home, (20)large pieces of cloth for domestic use and fabrics needed for manufacturing began to be dyed by professionals.

Questions
Item 1
  A. People have always color fabrics with dyes.
  B. People always did color fabrics with dyes.
  C. People have always colored fabrics with dyes.
  D. People have always colored, fabrics with dyes.
  E. People always color fabrics with dyes.

Item 2
  A. People use to get dyes
  B. People got dyes
  C. People use to got dyes
  D. People used to get dyes
  E. People use dyes
Item 3
  A. from those plants they found around them
  B. from the plants they found around them
  C. from some plants they found around them
  D. from the plants, they found around them
  E. from plants, they found around them

Item 4
  A. and variously techniques for dyeing
  B. and often techniques for dyeing
  C. and different techniques for dying
  D. and different techniques for dyeing
  E. and various dying techniques

Item 5
  A. dyeing in Europe were craft skills
  B. dyeing in Europe were skills
  C. dyeing in Europe were crafts
  D. dyeing in Europe was a craft skill
  E. dyeing in Europe is a craft skill

Item 6
  A. gained by lengthy apprenticeship
  B. gained by longer apprenticeship
  C. gaining a long apprenticeship
  D. for which one gained a long apprenticeship
  E. and gained lengthy apprenticeship

Item 7
  A. materials which came from plants, minerals, and animals
  B. materials, which came from plants, minerals, and animals
  C. materials; which came from plants, minerals, and animals
  D. materials: which came from plants, minerals, and animals
  E. materials from plants, minerals, and animals

Item 8
- A. Manufacturing natural dyes required much skill
- B. Manufacturing natural dyes required many skill
- C. Manufacturing natural dyes required more skill
- D. Manufacturing natural dyes was in need of much skill
- E. Manufacturing natural dyes required too much skill

Item 9
- A. Indigo is maybe the oldest natural dye.
- B. Maybe indigo is the oldest natural dye.
- C. Indigo maybe is the oldest natural dye.
- D. May indigo be the oldest natural dye.
- E. Indigo is probably the oldest natural dye.

Item 10
- A. the dye comprises only 1/2% of the plant's weight.
- B. the dye composes only 1/2% of the plant's weight.
- C. the dye consists of only 1/2% of the plant's weight.
- D. the dye is comprising of only 1/2% of the plant's weight.
- E. the dye contains only 1/2% of the plant's weight.

Item 11
- A. Lots of species of three different plant families
- B. Many species of three different plant families
- C. Lots of species in three different plant families
- D. Lots of different plant families
- E. Every species of three different plant families

Item 12
- A. but tropical were especially prized
- B. but tropical varieties were especially prized
- C. but tropical kind were especially prized
- D. but, tropical ones were especially prized
- E. but tropical ones, were especially prized

Item 13
- A. From India and Africa, for example, came the best indigo.
- B. From India and Africa, for example, the best indigo came.
- C. The best indigo came from India and Africa, for example.
- D. For example, came the best indigo from India and Africa.
- E. For example, there came the best indigo from India and Africa.

Item 14
    A. Native Americans were for long expert dyers before the arrival of Europeans.
    B. Native Americans were long expert dyers before the arrival of Europeans.
    C. Native Americans for long were expert dyers before the arrival of Europeans.
    D. Native Americans were expert dyers long before the arrival of Europeans.
    E. Long before the arrival of Europeans were Native Americans expert dyers.

Item 15
    A. used their dyes and methods they brought from Europe
    B. used their dyes and methods that they brought from Europe
    C. used the dyes and methods they brought from Europe
    D. used they're dyes and methods from Europe
    E. used there dyes and methods from Europe

Item 16
    A. but over time they turned to dyes
    B. but, over time they turned to dyes
    C. but over time they used dyes
    D. but over time, they turned to dyes
    E. but over time they turned into dyes

Item 17
    A. to supplant those imported from Europe
    B. to supply those imported from Europe
    C. to preserve those imported from Europe
    D. to supplicate those imported from Europe
    E. to supplement those imported from Europe

Item 18
    A. dyeing becomes a specialized skill
    B. dyeing became a specialized skill
    C. dyeing did become a specialized skill
    D. dyeing once became a specialized skill
    E. dyeing became one specialized skill

Item 19
    A. sometimes moves outside the home to a special site
    B. sometimes is moved outside the home to a special site
    C. sometimes had moved outside the home to a special site
    D. sometimes moved outside the home to a special site
    E. sometimes did move outside the home to a special site

Item 20
- A. large pieces of cloth for domestic use and fabrics needed for manufacturing began to be dyed by professionals
- B. large pieces of cloth, for domestic use, and fabrics, needed for manufacturing, began to be dyed by professionals
- C. large pieces of cloth for domestic use, and fabrics needed for manufacturing began to be dyed by professionals
- D. large pieces of cloth for domestic use, and fabrics needed for manufacturing, began to be dyed by professionals
- E. large pieces of cloth for domestic use and fabrics, needed for manufacturings began to be dyed by professionals

Passage 2 – Spanish Town

(21)Spanish Town is the most old neighborhood in Baton Rouge. (22)It was founded in 1805, two years after the Louisiana Purchase. (23)It was part of the "Province of West Florida" and contained many people of English ancestry, and they disliked Spanish rule. They really wanted to be part of America rather than Spain. (24)They started a rebellion which managed to break away from Spain in 1810.

(25)People came from the Canary Islands settled along what is now called Spanish Town Road in 1805. (26)The Canary Islands located off the coast of North Africa. (27)The Canary Islanders were Spanish heritage, unlike the English residents. By living in "Spanish Town," (28)they could keep their own identity, their Spanish language and community.

Spanish Town (29)is still a unique community today—a sense of difference. The people who live there (30)maybe aren't the richest people in Baton Rouge. However, (31)they are interesting including (32)artists, writers, and musicians. (33)Doctors live here too, and lawyers. (34)Many college students are renting apartments here. A wide range of income-levels, from poor to quite wealthy, (35)are found in the neighborhood. You can see grand mansions next to shotgun houses, (36)small houses that is one room wide and several rooms deep. (37)Whatever size they are nearly all of these houses display pink flamingos. This pink flamingo is the neighborhood mascot, (38)symbolizing the neighborhood's unity and (39)sense of individualness.

Indeed, (40)the residents of Spanish Town think themselves different from the rest of Baton Rouge. They take pride in their narrow streets, historic homes with front porches, stray cats, and diverse people.

<u>Questions</u>

Item 21
- A. Spanish Town is the most old neighborhood
- B. Spanish Town is the most oldest neighborhood
- C. Spanish Town is the older neighborhood
- D. Spanish Town is the oldest neighborhood
- E. Spanish Town is the old neighborhood

Item 22
- A. It was founded in 1805,
- B. Founded in 1805,
- C. It were founded in 1805,
- D. They founded it in 1805,
- E. It was found in 1805,

Item 23
- A. It was part of the "Province of West Florida" and contained many people of English ancestry, and they disliked Spanish rule.
- B. It was part of the "Province of West Florida" and contained many people of English ancestry. They disliked Spanish rule.
- C. It was part of the "Province of West Florida," and contained many people of English ancestry, and they disliked Spanish rule.
- D. It was part of the "Province of West Florida," and contained many people of English ancestry, who disliked Spanish rule.
- E. It was part of the "Province of West Florida" and there were many people of English ancestry, and they disliked Spanish rule.

Item 24
- A. They started a rebellion which managed to break away from Spain
- B. They started a rebellion that managed to break away from Spain
- C. They started a rebellion, and managed to break away from Spain
- D. They started a rebellion when they managed to break away from Spain
- E. They started a rebellion and managed to break away from Spain

Item 25
- A. People came from the Canary Islands settled along what is now called Spanish Town Road
- B. People came from the Canary Islands they settled along what is now called Spanish Town Road
- C. People which came from the Canary Islands settled along what is now called Spanish Town Road
- D. People from the Canary Islands settled along what is now called Spanish Town Road
- E. People came from the Canary Islands to settled along what is now called Spanish Town Road

- 137 -

Item 26
   A. The Canary Islands located off the coast
   B. The Canary Islands were located off the coast
   C. The Canary Islands are located off the coast
   D. The Canary Islands, located off the coast
   E. The Canary Islands located the coast

Item 27
   A. The Canary Islanders were Spanish heritage
   B. The Canary Islanders were of Spanish heritage
   C. The Canary Islanders had Spanish heritage
   D. The Canary Islanders did Spanish heritage
   E. The Canary Islanders are Spanish heritage

Item 28
   A. they could keep their own identity, their Spanish language and community.
   B. they could keep their own identity their Spanish language and community.
   C. they could keep their own identity, and their Spanish language, and community.
   D. they could keep their own identity Spanish, their language and community.
   E. they could keep their own identity, their Spanish language, and community.

Item 29
   A. is still a unique community today—a sense of difference
   B. is still a unique community today with a sense of difference
   C. is still a unique community today in a sense of difference
   D. is still a unique community today: a sense of difference
   E. is still a unique community today, one with a sense of difference

Item 30
   A. maybe aren't the richest people
   B. are perhaps not the richest people
   C. aren't maybe the richest people
   D. maybe are not the richest people
   E. are not the richest people perhaps

Item 31
   A. they are interesting including
   B. they are interesting and including
   C. they are interesting and include
   D. they are interesting, and include
   E. they are interestingly including

Item 32
    A. artists, writers, and musicians
    B. artists, writers and musicians
    C. artists, and writers, and musicians
    D. artists and writers, and musicians
    E. artists writers, and musicians

Item 33
    A. Doctors live here too, and lawyers.
    B. Doctors live here too, and lawyers live here.
    C. Doctors and lawyers also live here too.
    D. Doctors also live here, too, and lawyers.
    E. Doctors live here too, and also lawyers.

Item 34
    A. Many college students are renting apartments here.
    B. Many college students do rent apartments, here.
    C. College students are renting many apartments here.
    D. Many college students rent apartments here.
    E. Many college students are here rent apartments.

Item 35
    A. are found in the neighborhood
    B. are to be found in the neighborhood
    C. is found in the neighborhood
    D. are available in the neighborhood
    E. are in the neighborhood

Item 36
    A. small houses that is one room wide
    B. small house that is one room wide
    C. small house one room wide
    D. small houses that are one room wide
    E. small houses that will be one room wide

Item 37
    A. Whatever size they are nearly all of these houses display pink flamingos.
    B. Whatever size they are, nearly all of these houses display pink flamingos.
    C. Whatever size they are nearly all these houses display pink flamingos.
    D. Whatever size they may be nearly all of these houses display pink flamingos.
    E. Whatever size they are all of these houses display pink flamingos.

Item 38
- A. symbolizing the neighborhood's unity
- B. symbolizing the neighborhood's unification
- C. symbolizing the neighborhoods unity
- D. remonstrating the neighborhood's unity
- E. symbolizing Spanish Town's unity

Item 39
- A. sense of individualness
- B. sense of oneness
- C. sense of togetherness
- D. sense of uniqueness
- E. sense of cohesion

Item 40
- A. the residents of Spanish Town think themselves different
- B. the residents of Spanish Town think of themselves different
- C. the residents of Spanish Town think themselves as different
- D. the residents of Spanish Town think themselves differently
- E. the residents of Spanish Town think themselves indifferent

Passage 3 – Poe

Edgar Allan Poe (41)was birthed in Boston on January 19, 1809. (42)His parents was David Poe and Elizabeth Arnold Hopkins. David Poe was a heavy drinker ((43)as were both Edgar and his older brother William) and eventually left the family. Elizabeth had little time to be a mother, (44)pursuing an acting career and the stress of supporting three young children. (45)She died suddenly of Tuberculosis (46)at only the age of only 24.

(47)Edgar describes the impact of never having known loving parents in (48)a letter to Beverley Tucker, which he wrote it in 1835. Tucker had known Poe's mother, (49)and Poe wrote to her "In speaking of my mother you have touched a string to which my heart fully responds. ... I have many occasional dealings with adversity — (50)but the want of parental affection has been the heaviest of my trials". (51)Poe shows a persistant need for female attention and love, (52)a theme that recurring throughout his life but also in many of his literary works.

The young (53)Edgar was taken eventually in by John and Francis Allan. Francis spoiled him, providing for his material needs. And yet, she was seldom available to him, for like his natural mother, (54)she was too ill to do. (55)Her poor health added only to young Edgar's misery.

(56)A desultory female friend to Poe in his early life was Mrs. Jane Stith Stanard. (57)The mother of Poe's classmate, Robert Stanard. She was in her thirties. (58)Mrs. Stanard, who Poe called Helen, was always (59)<u>sympathetic to the 14 year old Edgar</u>. Unfortunately, Mrs. Stanard, too, was in poor health, and in the spring of 1824 (60)<u>she suddenly fell seriously ill, and she died on April 28th.</u> Her death added to Poe's desperation and grief. In 1848 he wrote the poem, To Helen, as an expression of his love for her.

<u>Questions</u>

Item 41

- A. was birthed in Boston
- B. has been borne in Boston
- C. has been born in Boston
- D. was borne in Boston
- E. was born in Boston

Item 42

- A. His parents was David Poe and Elizabeth Arnold Hopkins.
- B. His parent's were David Poe and Elizabeth Arnold Hopkins.
- C. His parents were David Poe and Elizabeth Arnold Hopkins.
- D. His parent's was David Poe and Elizabeth Arnold Hopkins.
- E. His Parents were David Poe and Elizabeth Arnold Hopkins.

Item 43

- A. as were both Edgar and his older brother William
- B. as were, both, Edgar and his older brother William
- C. as were both, Edgar and his older brother William
- D. as both Edgar and his older brother William were
- E. so were both Edgar and his older brother William

Item 44

- A. pursuing an acting career and the stress of supporting three young children
- B. pursuing an acting career and stressed by supporting three young children
- C. pursuing an acting career and stressed out with supporting three young children
- D. pursuing an acting career and the stress of three young children
- E. pursuing an acting career and the three young children

Item 45

- A. She died suddenly of Tuberculosis
- B. She died, suddenly, of Tuberculosis
- C. She died suddenly of tuberculosis
- D. She died of Tuberculosis suddenly
- E. She suddenly died of Tuberculosis

Item 46
- A. at only the age of only 24
- B. at only the age of 24
- C. at the age of only 24
- D. at the age of 24
- E. at the only age of 24

Item 47
- A. Edgar describes the impact
- B. Edgar described the impact
- C. Edgar is describing the impact
- D. Edgar had described the impact
- E. Edgar was described the impact

Item 48
- A. a letter to Beverley Tucker, which he wrote it in 1835
- B. a letter to Beverley Tucker which he wrote it in 1835
- C. a letter to Beverley Tucker, which he wrote in 1835
- D. a letter to Beverley Tucker which was wrote in 1835
- E. a letter to Beverley Tucker; which he wrote in 1835

Item 49
- A. and Poe wrote to her
- B. and Poe wrote to her;
- C. and Poe wrote to her—
- D. and Poe wrote to her:
- E. and Poe wrote to her…

Item 50
- A. but the want of parental affection
- B. but the abundance of parental affection
- C. but the wanting of parental affection
- D. but the whim of parental affection
- E. but the disinterest of parental affection

Item 51
- A. Poe shows a persistant need
- B. Poe shows an importunate need
- C. Poe shows a timeless need
- D. Poe shows a persistent need
- E. Poe shows a constructive need

Item 52
    A. a theme that recurring throughout his life
    B. a theme recurring throughout his life
    C. a theme that recurs throughout his life
    D. a theme that is recurring throughout his life
    E. a theme recurring not only throughout his life

Item 53
    A. Edgar was taken eventually in by
    B. Edgar was taken finally in by
    C. Edgar was taken ultimately in by
    D. Edgar was taken in eventually by
    E. Edgar was taken in amorphously by

Item 54
    A. she was too ill to do.
    B. she was too ill to.
    C. she was too ill to do so.
    D. she was to ill to do.
    E. she was to ill.

Item 55
    A. Her poor health added only to young Edgar's misery.
    B. Only her poor health added to young Edgar's misery.
    C. Her poor health only added to young Edgar's misery.
    D. Her poor health added to only young Edgar's misery.
    E. Her poor health added to young Edgar's only misery.

Item 56
    A. A desultory female friend to Poe in his early life
    B. A misogynous female friend to Poe in his early life
    C. A capricious female friend to Poe in his early life
    D. A prominent female friend to Poe in his early life
    E. A congratulatory female friend to Poe in his early life

Item 57
    A. The mother of Poe's classmate, Robert Stanard. She was in her thirties.
    B. The mother of Poe's classmate, Robert Stanard; she was in her thirties.
    C. The mother of Poe's classmate, Robert Stanard: she was in her thirties.
    D. The mother of Poe's classmate, Robert Stanard: She was in her thirties.
    E. The mother of Poe's classmate, Robert Stanard, she was in her thirties.

Item 58

    A. Mrs. Stanard, who Poe called Helen,

    B. Mrs. Stanard who Poe called Helen

    C. Mrs. Stanard, who called Poe Helen,

    D. Mrs. Stanard, whom Poe called Helen,

    E. Mrs. Stanard, whom was called Helen by Poe,

Item 59

    A. sympathetic to the 14 year old Edgar

    B. sympathetic to the 14-year-old Edgar

    C. sympathetic to the 14-year old Edgar

    D. sympathetic to the 14 year-old Edgar

    E. pleasant to the 14 year old Edgar

Item 60

    A. she suddenly fell seriously ill, and she died on April 28th.

    B. she suddenly fell seriously ill. She died on April 28th.

    C. she suddenly fell seriously ill, and then she died on April 28th.

    D. she suddenly fell seriously ill, and finally she died on April 28th.

    E. she suddenly fell seriously ill, when she died on April 28th.

Answer Explanations

Reading Test Answers

Reading Passage 1

1. The correct answer is B. The passage gives general instructions for tomato plant culture from seeding to providing support for the vines. Answers A and D are too specific, focusing on details of the text. Answer C is too general: the passage does not fully describe how to operate a farm.
2. The correct answer is C. The passage states that seeds germinated in late March will be ready for the garden after the last frost.
3. The correct answer is A. . The passage states that seeds germinated in late March will be ready for the garden after the last frost, implying that exposure to freezing temperatures would harm them.
4. The correct answer is E. The text describes a sequence of window boxes followed by pots and finally outdoor planting.
5. The correct answer is A. The text states that pinching the bud is done to make the plants stronger.
6. The correct answer is B. Larger plants have longer roots and require more soil and water for nourishment.
7. The correct answer is C. The text states that the cloth is used to protect the soil. We can infer that this is because a stream of water may disrupt it and uproot the seedlings.
8. The correct answer is E. Manure is added to the potting mix and to the final soil. Nitrate of soda is suggested as an additive to the garden soil to give the plants "a good start".
9. The correct answer is A. The text states that use of fresh manure will delay fruiting.
10. The correct answer is D. The text indicates that unsupported plants flop on the ground. The support system spreads the vines, giving the fruit more room. Thus, the plants require more space and ust be planted further apart.
11. The correct answer is D. Although all the other answers make mention of information contained in the paragraph, the overall purpose of this paragraph is as stated, to describe the support procedure.
12. The correct answer is C. The last sentence tells us that training of the plants, or supporting them, should begin before they trail on the ground.

Reading Passage 2

13. The correct answer is D. The passage describes the artistry of Greek coinage and gives the reasons why so much effort went into designing them.
14. The correct answer is B. The first sentence shows that the author thinks of coins as utilitarian objects and that few of them are designed in a manner that makes them worth considering as something more than that.

15. The correct answer is A. "Delectation" means to savor or to enjoy the flavor or beauty of something, in this case the design of the coins.
16. The correct answer is D. The word is defined in passing in the text in the second sentence.
17. The correct answer is E. The passage describes the coins as artistic objects, not simply because they were the first coins, but also because of the historical situation which is described, and which led to their being designed with great care and pride.
18. The correct answer is C. The text states that new coins were developed frequently, to commemorate battles, treaties, etc.
19. The correct answer is A. The text tells us that the designers were highly skilled and that they were so proud of their work that they signed it.
20. The correct answer is E. The sentence contrasts the artistic content of the coins with their use as a practical means of commercial exchange.
21. The correct answer is D. The text tells us that coin designs changed along with larger sculptures to reflect changing Greek artistic tastes.
22. The correct answer is B. The frequent need for new designs meant that the artisans who did the work had ample opportunity to perfect their skills.
23. The correct answer is C. The text tells us that the dated coins provide a dependable record of Greek artistic development.
24. The correct answer is D. Coins were developed as a means of commercial exchange, and the text tells us that this was their main use.

Reading Passage 3

25. The correct answer is C. In the first sentence the phrase "so long had sleep been denied her" tells us she had been prevented from sleeping for some time.
26. The correct answer is D. The text tells us she was feigning, which means to pretend, to be asleep.
27. The correct answer is A. Despite his ugliness and deformity, Garth is a gentle soul who wants to be accepted as a friend by the girl.
28. The correct answer is E. AT first repelled by the sight of Garth in the window, the girl eventually expresses pity when she learns that he is deaf, too.
29. The correct answer is C. Garth's deformities are repugnant to her at first, and she must overcome this emotion.
30. The correct answer is B. He calls back to her that he is hidden from sight, and his voice is described as plaintive and pained.
31. The correct answer is B. The text tells us that he sees her lips move and assumes she is sending him away, because he cannot hear that she is calling to him.
32. The correct answer is D.
33. The correct answer is D. At first she was amazed at the extent of Garth;s deformities, but she has quickly become more sympathetic and has come to pity him
34. The correct answer is E. The girl quickly understands Garth's sadness about his own condition and sympathizes with him.

35. The correct answer is C. Garth is sad that he is so deformed that other people are frequently repelled and try to avoid contact with him.

36. The correct answer is D. The girl has shown that she sympathizes with him by taking his arm, and Garth feels that he is being accepted despite his deformities.

Reading Passage 4

37. The correct answer is C. An archipelago is a large group or chain of islands.

38. The correct answer is D. The article deals primarily with the ways the colonists fed themselves: their crops and the foods they hunted. While it also describes New Zealand's prehistory, the main focus is on food sources.

39. The correct answer is B. The article states that the islands were colonized by Polynesians in the fifteenth century but that the first settlers had arrived some 400 years earlier than that.

40. The correct answer is E. The passage states that the first settlers were forced to rely on fishing for their food.

41. The correct answer is A. When an increased population had driven a major food source to extinction, they began to fight for control over the remaining food supply.

42. The correct answer is D. The article tells us that coconuts did not grow in New Zealand, and that some of the other crops would grow only on North Island.

43. The correct answer is C. The sweet potato could be stored, providing a source of food during the winter when other food gathering activities were difficult.

44. The correct answer is A. The sweet potato provided a winter food source through storage, allowing the population to increase.

45. The correct answer is E. All of the reasons given are good ones for locating the camps near the source of food production.

46. The correct answer is E. As the human population increased, they depleted many of their food source faster than the populations could reproduce and renew themselves.

47. The correct answer is E. The moa were flightless birds, so they could not easily escape when the humans came to hunt them.

48. The correct answer is A. The Maori turned to cannibalism after the moa disappeared and they had lost a major source of food and protein.

Reading Passage 5

49. The correct answer is C. The passage describes several distinctive features of annelid anatomy and tells how some of them differ from other worms.

50. The correct answer is A. The term is defined in the text as an organization of the anatomy into segments.

51. The correct answer is E. The term is defined in the text between commas.

52. The correct answer is C. The text gives the example of feet specializing into grasping organs to illustrate this evolutionary advantage of segmental plasticity.

53. The correct answer is B. *Nematodes* differ from the annelids in the structure of the coelum. *Lumbricus* and leeches are both members of the Annelida.

54. The correct answer is E. The text gives the example of parapodia modified for grasping to illustrate evolutionary plasticity among metameres.

55. The correct answer is B. The text states that the annelid coelum is formed later during embryology and probably evolved at a later time, as well.

56. The correct answer is E. The text indicates that the cerebral ganglia are enlarged, whereas the remaining ganglia in the nerve cord are merely repeating (unspecialized) units.

57. The correct answer is C. The text defines metemeres as segments, and discusses segmentation as the distinguishing feature of the phylum.

58. The correct answer is D. The paragraph tells us that annelids can live in salt or fresh water and on land, and then gives examples.

59. The correct answer is E. The text indicates that both nematodes and annelids possess a fluid-filled cavity which is involved in locomotion, or movement.

60. The correct answer is E. The last paragraph indicates that annelids occupy all the habitats listed and gives examples.

Math Test Answers

Numerical Skills / Prealgebra

1. B: The order of operations dictates that addition and subtraction be computed as each appears, from left to right, in the expression. Thus, the expression can first be rewritten as $18 + 7 + 5 + 11$. The expression can next be rewritten as $25 + 5 + 11$. Finally, the expression can be rewritten as $30 + 11$, which equals 41.

2. D: The following expression can be used to represent the problem: $5.50 - (3.25 + 2.00) + 3.50$. The order of operations requires that the computation within parentheses be handled first. Thus, the expression can be rewritten as $5.50 - 5.25 + 3.50$. The expression can next be rewritten as $0.25 + 3.50$, which equals 3.75. So, Luis had \$3.75 in his wallet at the end of the day.

3. A: The order of operations dictates that any computations within parentheses be first calculated. Thus, the expression can be rewritten as $\frac{1}{3} + \frac{2}{15} - \frac{2}{15}$. The additive inverse property reveals that the last two terms in the expression sum to 0, leaving $\frac{1}{3}$ as the answer.

4. E: The problem requires 13.71 feet of wire be subtracted from the total number of feet purchased, or 14.5 feet. The difference is 0.79. John had 0.79 feet of wire left over after fixing the lamp.

5. D: A non-member must pay $12 × 7, or $84, for all 7 CDs. A member pays $24 for all 7 CDs. Thus, Maria saves $84 − $24, or $60, by joining the club.

6. A: The difference is equal to 7,576,000. This number can be written in scientific notation by moving the decimal point behind the 7, in the millions place, and counting the number of digits to the right of the decimal point. The number, written in scientific notation, is 7.576×10^6.

7. D: The inequality can be rewritten as $3 < \sqrt{x} < 5$. Each term in the inequality can be squared, in order to eliminate the square root symbol. Thus, the inequality can be written as $(3)^2 < \left(\sqrt{x}\right)^2 < (5)^2$, or $9 < x < 25$.

8. D: The rule of exponents states that $x^{\frac{a}{b}} = \sqrt[b]{x^a}$. Thus, $\sqrt[3]{27} = 27^{\frac{1}{3}}$, or 3. Thus, the product can be written as 3×3, or 9.

9. B: A proportion in the form $\frac{a}{b} = \frac{c}{d}$ can be rewritten as $ad = bc$. Thus, the given proportion can be solved for x as follows: $11x = 49$, where $x = \frac{49}{11}$.

10. C: The problem can be represented by the proportion, $\frac{12}{\$48.75} = \frac{13}{x}$. The solution is equal to $\frac{\$48.75 \times 13}{12}$, or $\frac{13}{12} \times \$48.75$.

11. E: The number of people who passed the exam is equal to 0.80×55, or 44. Since 55 people took the exam, the number of people who failed the exam is equal to $55 − 44$, or 11.

12. C: In order to convert the fraction, $\frac{3}{4}$, into a percent, the fraction must first be converted to a decimal. In order to do so, the denominator of the fraction must be divided into its numerator; $3 \div 4 = 0.75$. The decimal, 0.75, can be converted to a percent by moving the decimal point two places to the right. Thus, 75% of the participants crossed the finish line in less than 3 hours.

13. C: Since the first three SAT scores summed to 1900, the following equation can be used to find the score on the fourth exam: $\frac{1900+x}{4} = 650$. The equation can be solved for x by multiplying both sides of the equation by 4. Doing so gives: $1900 + x = 2600$. Subtracting 1900 from both sides of the equation gives $x = 700$. Thus, he scored 700 on his fourth SAT exam.

14. C: The average time can be represented by the expression, $\frac{3}{4}(16) + \frac{1}{4}(12)$, which equals the sum of 12 and 3, or 15. Thus, the average time overall was 15 seconds.

15. B: Since she made $21 in commissions during the first 3 hours, the following equation can be used to find the dollar amount she must make during the fourth hour: $\frac{\$21+x}{4} = \$8$. The equation can be solved for x by multiplying both sides of the equation by 4. Doing so gives: $\$21 + x = \$32$.

Subtracting $21 from both sides of the equation gives $x = \$11$. Thus, she must make $11, in commissions, during the fourth hour, in order to average $8 per hour for the full four hours.

Algebra

16. B: The evaluation of the equation, for an x-value of -2, gives the following: $y = \frac{(-2)^4 - 2}{(-2)^2 + 1}$, which reduces to $y = \frac{16 - 2}{4 + 1}$, or $y = \frac{14}{5}$. The improper fraction, $\frac{14}{5}$, can also be written as the mixed number, $2\frac{4}{5}$. Thus, $y = 2\frac{4}{5}$.

17. B: The BMI for the given person can be written as $BMI = \frac{4.88 \times 110}{(5)^2}$, or $BMI = \frac{536.8}{25}$, or approximately 21.5.

18. D: The translated expression is $2\left(h \cdot \frac{r^2}{V}\right)$, which reduces to $\frac{2hr^2}{V}$.

19. E: The situation can be represented by the slope of 18, since the cost of renting equipment is $18 per day, for x days. The y-intercept is 48 because a member must pay a $48 membership fee, regardless of whether or not ski equipment is rented. Thus, the situation can be represented by the linear equation, $y = 18x + 48$.

20. E: The minus symbol in front of the parentheses can first be distributed, giving: $3x + 5y - 2y + 7x$, which reduces to $10x + 3y$.

21. C: The sum of the polynomials can be written as: $5x^2 - 4x + 1 - 3x^2 + x - 3$, which reduces to $2x^2 - 3x - 2$.

22. D: The polynomial can be factored as $(x - 7)(x + 3)$. Thus, $(x - 7)$ is a factor of the given polynomial.

23. B: The product given for Choice B can be written as $27x^3 - 9x^2y + 3xy^2 + 9x^2y - 3xy^2 + y^3$, which reduces to $27x^3 + y^3$.

24. A: The temperature conversion formula, evaluated for 18 degrees Celsius, can be written as $F = \frac{9(18)}{5} + 32$, which equals $F = \frac{162}{5} + 32$, or $F = 64.4$. The Fahrenheit equivalent is 64.4 degrees.

25. E: The equation can be solved for x by first subtracting $0.75x$ from both sides. Doing so gives: $-0.25x = -2$. Dividing both sides by -0.25 gives $x = 8$.

26. C: The rules of exponents can be applied in order to rewrite the expression as: $-4q^3r^2s^{-1}$, which equals $\frac{-4q^3r^2}{s}$, or $-4\frac{q^3r^2}{s}$.

27. D: The radical expression can be rewritten as $\dfrac{\sqrt{x^4}}{\sqrt{y^5}}$, which equals $\dfrac{x^2}{\sqrt{y^4}\sqrt{y}}$ or $\dfrac{x^2}{y^2\sqrt{y}}$.

28. E: When dividing terms with identical bases, the exponents are to be subtracted, i.e., $\dfrac{a^4}{a^3} = a^1$ or a. Thus, the rational expression can be rewritten $a^{11}b^{-15}c^{-2}$. The rules of exponents also state: $a^{-x} = \dfrac{1}{a^x}$. So, the rational expression can now be rewritten as $\dfrac{a^{11}}{b^{15}c^2}$.

29. A: A line, given in the form, $y = mx + b$, has m as the slope and b as the y-intercept. In the linear equation, $y = 17x - 4$, 17 is the slope of the line.

30. C: The linear equation can be rewritten as $y = -\dfrac{2}{3}x + \dfrac{7}{3}$. The slope-intercept form of an equation, or $y = mx + b$, includes m as the slope and b as the y-intercept. Therefore, the y-intercept of the equation is $\dfrac{7}{3}$.

College Algebra

31. C: The common ratio of the geometric sequence is –2. Therefore, the next term in the sequence will be the product of –16 and –2 or 32.

32. A: Evaluating the equation for the given principal, interest rate, and time gives:
$I = (15,000)(0.03)(2)$, or $I = 900$. The interest paid is $900.

33. C: The problem requires composition of the functions, whereby the function, $f(x)$, is evaluated within the function, $g(x)$. Therefore, the function, $g(x)$, is evaluated for an x-value, equal to the function, $f(x)$. The composition of function can be written as $g(f(x)) = \dfrac{2x+1}{3}$; $g(f(4)) = \dfrac{2(4)+1}{3}$, or 3.

34. D: The radical expression can be rewritten as the product, $\sqrt[3]{8x^3y^6}\sqrt[3]{x^2y}$, which simplifies to $2xy^2\sqrt[3]{x^2y}$. This product can be rewritten as $2xy^2(x^2y)^{\frac{1}{3}}$, or $2xy^2\left(x^{\frac{2}{3}}y^{\frac{1}{3}}\right)$. Multiplying the two expressions gives $2x^{\frac{5}{3}}y^{\frac{7}{3}}$.

35. C: When subtracting A from B, the difference matrix can be written as $\begin{bmatrix} 1-1 & -3-(-3) \\ -4-(-4) & 2-(-2) \end{bmatrix}$, which reduces to $\begin{bmatrix} 0 & 0 \\ 0 & 4 \end{bmatrix}$.

36. A: The difference of the functions can be written as $x^2 + 9x + 21 - (2(x + 5)^2)$. The expression can be rewritten by finding the product of the squared binomial. Thus, the difference of the functions can be written as $x^2 + 9x + 21 - (2(x^2 + 10x + 25))$. Distributing the 2 across the trinomial gives: $x^2 + 9x + 21 - (2x^2 + 20x + 50)$. Distributing the minus sign across the trinomial gives: $x^2 + 9x + 21 - 2x^2 - 20x - 50$. Collection of like terms gives: $-x^2 - 11x - 29$. Thus, the equivalent form of $f(x) - g(x)$ is $-x^2 - 11x - 29$.

- 151 -

37. C: The problem requires composition of the functions, whereby the function, $g(x)$, is evaluated within the function, $f(x)$. Therefore, the function, $f(x)$, is evaluated for an x-value, equal to the function, $g(x)$. The composition of function can be written as $f(g(x)) = 2(x^2 + 5) + 6$, which simplifies to $f(g(x)) = 2x^2 + 10 + 6$, or $f(g(x)) = 2x^2 + 16$; $f(g(6)) = 2(6)^2 + 16$, or 88.

38. B: The product is equal to $-14\square^2$. Since $\square^2 = -1$, the product can be rewritten as $(-14)(-1)$, or 14.

39. E: The equation, $y = \frac{k}{x}$, represents the inverse variation of y with x, for some constant, k. The given x- and y-values from the first portion of the problem, can be used to find the constant, k; $-6 = \frac{k}{14}$. Solving for k gives: $k = -84$. This k-value and the given y-value, in the second portion of the problem, can be used to find the x-value, given the y-value of -11; $-11 = \frac{-84}{x}$; multiplying both sides of the equation by x gives: $-11x = -84$, where $x = \frac{-84}{-11}$, or $7\frac{7}{11}$.

40. D: The difference matrix can be written as $[0.2 - 2 \quad 3.2 - 1.7 \quad -4.1 - 1.9]$, which simplifies to $[-1.8 \quad 1.5 \quad -6]$.

Geometry

41. E: The area of the rectangular wall is equal to the product of the length, 17, and height, 12, or 204 square feet. The area of one of the circular windows can be written as $= \pi(2)^2$, or 4π, which is approximately 12.56 square feet; the approximate area of two circular windows is equal to the product of 2 and 12.56, or 25.12 square feet. The approximate remaining area, or the area to be painted, is equal to the difference of 204 square feet and 25.12 square feet, or 178.88 square feet. Since 1 quart of paint is needed for every 10 square feet of wall area, the following proportion can be written: $\frac{1}{10} = \frac{x}{178.88}$; solving for x gives $x \approx 17.89$, or 18.

42. C: Since $\overline{DE}$ bisects angle ACB, angles ACD and BCD, each equal 40°; note that the isosceles triangle has base angles of 50°, revealing the measure of angle ACB to be 80°. Since angle ACD and angle ACE are supplementary angles, the measure of angle ACE is equal to the difference of 180° and 40°, or 140°.

43. E: The problem describes an inscribed circle, within a square. Since the square has side lengths of a, the diameter of the circle is also a. The length of the track is synonymous with the circumference of the track, which can be represented by the equation, $C = \pi d$; substituting a for d gives: $C = \pi a$. Thus, the length of the track is πa.

44. B: The length of $\overline{AB}$ can be determined by applying the Pythagorean Theorem, which states $a^2 + b^2 = c^2$, where a and b represent legs of a right triangle, and c represents the hypotenuse.

Substituting the lengths of BC and hypotenuse, AC, into the equation gives: $a^2 + 12^2 = 13^2$ or $a^2 + 144 = 169$. Solving for a gives: $a^2 = 25$, or $a = 5$. Thus, the length of AB is 5 ft.

45. B: The length of an arc is proportional to the measure of the arc, relative to the circle. Here, the length of arc $\overset{\frown}{AB}$ is in a ratio of 4:48, or 1:12, with the total circle perimeter. Thus the measure of arc $\overset{\frown}{AB}$ has a ratio of 1:12 with the total circle measure, which is always 360°. To find the unknown arc measure, set up a proportion with the known information as follows: $\frac{1}{12} = \frac{x}{360°}$. Solving for x gives $12x = 360°$, or $x = 30°$.

46. E: The volume of a cylinder can be determined, by using the formula, $V = \pi r^2 h$, where r represents the radius of the cylinder and h represents the height. The volume of the aluminum can is equal to $\pi(2)^2 8$, or 32π, which is approximately 100.48. In order to find the necessary height of the glass jar, the radius of 1.5 inches and prior volume of the aluminum can need to be substituted into the volume formula; $100.48 = \pi(1.5)^2 h$, giving $100.48 = 2.25\pi h$. Solving for h gives: $h \approx 14.22$. The height of $14\frac{1}{4}$ inches, given for Choice E, is closest to this approximation.

47. A: Since the slope of the radius of the circle is $-\frac{6}{5}$, the slope of the tangent line is $\frac{5}{6}$, or the negative reciprocal of the slope of the radius. Using the given point on the circle and the slope of the tangent line, the equation of the tangent line can be written; $y - 6 = \frac{5}{6}(x + 5)$.

48. C: The Pythagorean Theorem can be applied, in order to find the lengths of the bases of the two right triangles; $3^2 + b^2 = 5^2$. Solving for b gives: $b^2 = 16$, where $b = 4$. Thus, the length of $\overline{AB}$, or b_1, is equal to the sum of 4, 6, and 4, or 14. The area of a trapezoid can be determined, by using the formula, $A = \frac{1}{2}(b_1 + b_2)h$. Substituting the base lengths of 14 and 6 and height of 3, into the formula, gives: $A = \frac{1}{2}(14 + 6)3$, or $A = \frac{1}{2}(60)$, which equals 30. Thus, the total area of the trapezoid is 30 square units.

49. A: Since each side of the square is a units and point E divides $\overline{CD}$ into two equivalent line segments, right triangles, ACE and BDE, have legs of length, a and $\frac{a}{2}$. Thus, the area of each right triangle, can be written as $A = \frac{1}{2}\left(\frac{a}{2}\right)(a)$, or $A = \frac{1}{2}\left(\frac{a^2}{2}\right)$, which reduces to $\frac{a^2}{4}$. The area of both right triangles is equal to the product of 2 and $\frac{a^2}{4}$, or $\frac{2a^2}{4}$, which reduces to $\frac{a^2}{2}$. The area of ΔBAE is equal to the difference of the area of the square and the sum of the two right triangles. Thus, the area of ΔBAE can be written as $a^2 - \frac{a^2}{2}$. Finding a least common denominator allows the expression to be written as $\frac{2a^2}{2} - \frac{a^2}{2}$, or $\frac{a^2}{2}$. So, the area of ΔBAE is $\frac{a^2}{2}$ square units.

50. A: The formula for the area of a circle relates to radius as follows: $= \pi(radius)^2$. Since $\frac{a}{A} = \frac{1}{4}$, substituting the expression in terms of radius yields: $\frac{\pi r^2}{\pi R^2} = \frac{1}{4}$. This reduces to $\frac{r^2}{R^2} = \frac{1}{4}$. Taking the

- 153 -

square root of both sides gives $\sqrt{\frac{r^2}{R^2}} = \sqrt{\frac{1}{4}}$, or $\frac{r}{R} = \frac{1}{2}$. Thus the ratio of the radii is 1:2 when the area has a ratio of 1:4.

51. D: The area of a sector of a circle can be determined by using the formula, $A = \frac{\theta r^2}{2}$, where θ is measured in radians, and r represents the radius of the circle. The given central angle measure must first be converted to radians. Degrees can be converted to radians by multiplying the given degrees by $\frac{\pi}{180\ radians}$. Thus, 145° can be represented, in radians, as $145° \cdot \frac{\pi}{180\ radians}$, or approximately 2.53 radians. Substituting the radian measure of the central angle and the given radius into the area of a sector formula gives: $A = \frac{2.53(4)^2}{2}$, or approximately 20.2. Thus, the best representation for the area of the sector of the circle is 20.2 cm².

Trigonometry

52. B: The reciprocal of the cosine function is the secant function; $cos\theta = \frac{adjacent}{hypotenuse}$; $sec\theta = \frac{hypotenuse}{adjacent}$.

53. D: From the equation, $cosA = \frac{2}{5}$, it can be discerned that the adjacent side is equal to 2, while the hypotenuse length is equal to 5. The Pythagorean Theorem can be used to find the other missing leg; $2^2 + b^2 = 5^2; 4 + b^2 = 25$. Solving for b gives: $b = \sqrt{21}$. Since b represents the opposite leg, $tanA = \frac{\sqrt{21}}{2}$.

54. B: Since angle ACB equals 30°, angle BAC equals 60°. The sine function can be used to find the length of BC: $sin60° = \frac{x}{13}$. Multiplying both sides by 13 gives: $13 \sin 60° = x$, or $x \approx 11.3$. Thus, the length of BC is approximately 11.3.

55. D: Since the interior angle measures of a triangle sum to 180°, the measure of angle BAC is equal to the difference of the sum of the two given angles and 180°; $180° - (90° + 30°) = 60°$.

56. B: The following equation can be written to solve for the distance from the point at which the sailor is standing to the top of the lighthouse: $sin5° = \frac{350}{x}$. Multiplying both sides of the equation by x gives: $xsin5° = 350$. Division of both sides of the equation by $sin5°$ gives $x \approx 4000.52$. Thus, the approximate distance, from the sailor to the lighthouse, is 4000 feet.

57. C: The range of the function, $cos\theta$, is all real numbers greater than or equal to −1 and less than or equal to 1. Thus, the minimum range value is −1.

58. D: In order to convert from degrees to radians, the degrees must be multiplied by $\frac{\pi \ radians}{180°}$. Thus $45°$ can be converted to radians by writing: $45° \cdot \frac{\pi \ radians}{180°}$, which equals $\frac{45\pi}{180°}$ or $\frac{1}{4}$; $\frac{1}{4}\pi$ can also be written as $\frac{\pi}{4}$.

59. A: The graph of $f(x) = 6\sin(x)$ reveals a maximum value of 6, within the given domain interval of $-2\pi < x < 2\pi$. The regular sine function $f(x) = \sin(x)$ has a range of -1 to 1; here the function is multiplied by a factor of 6 thus enlarging the range from -6 and 6 for the same domain. There are two maximums of 6 within that domain.

60. E: From the equation, $\sin\alpha = \frac{5}{18}$, it can be discerned that the length of the side opposite α is equal to 5, while the hypotenuse length is 18. Since $\cos\alpha = \frac{1}{3}$, and both functions have the hypotenuse length as the denominator, the cosine equation can be rewritten as $\cos\alpha = \frac{6}{18}$. Now, the adjacent side can be determined to be 6. Thus, $\tan\alpha = \frac{5}{6}$.

Writing Test Answers

Passage 1 – Dyes

1. The correct answer is C. This employs the past participle "have colored".
2. The correct answer is D, using the past tense of "to use".
3. The correct answer is B. The end of the sentence is not a separate clause and should not be separated by a comma.
4. The correct answer is D. "Dying" means to end life, while "dyeing" means to color a fabric. "Variously" is an adverb that should modify a verb, not the noun "techniques".
5. The correct answer is D. The subject is singular and the context calls for a verb in the past tense.
6. The correct answer is A.
7. The correct answer is B, which uses a comma to set off a subordinate clause.
8. The correct answer is A.
9. The correct answer is E. Choice A is slang.
10. The correct answer is B. "To comprise" means "to be composed of".
11. The correct answer is B. Choice A is slang.
12. The correct answer is B. Choices D and E have inappropriate commas.
13. The correct answer is C, which exhibits the standard word order of subject – verb – indirect object.
14. The correct answer is D, which reads most smoothly using the prepositional phrase "long before".
15. The correct answer is C. Choices A and B are awkwardly phrased.
16. The correct answer is A. Choice C changes the meaning of the sentence.
17. The correct answer is E. Since they were using native dyes "as well" as European ones, they were not supplanting the latter. "Supplant" means to replace.
18. The correct answer is B, using the past tense of the verb.
19. The correct answer is D, matching the tense of the first half of the sentence.
20. The correct answer is A. The compound subject should not be broken up by commas.

Passage 2 – Spanish Town

21. The correct answer is D, using the superlative form of the adjective.
22. The correct answer is A. Choice D is an awkward phrasing.
23. The correct answer is B. The original is a run-on sentence, as are all the other choices.
24. The correct answer is E. Choice C is incorrect because the portion of the sentence following the comma has no subject. Choices A and B are incorrect because it was the people, rather than the rebellion, that broke away form Spain.
25. The correct answer is D. .
26. The correct answer is C, with the verb in the present tense, since the islands are still in this location.

27. The correct answer is B.
28. The correct answer is E, which uses the series comma to separate the items of a list.
29. The correct answer is E. Choice B requires a comma to set off the modifying clause at the end of the sentence.
30. The correct answer is B. Choices A, C, and D are slang usage.
31. The correct answer is C. Since "they" is the subject of both verbs ("are" and "include"), the comma in choice D is incorrect.
32. The correct answer is A, in which the series comma is used to separate the items of a list.
33. The correct answer is A. Choice B is awkward, and in the other choices "too" and "also", meaning the same thing, are redundant.
34. The correct answer is D, which uses the simple present tense of the verb.
35. The correct answer is C. The subject "a wide range," is singular, and the verb must also be singular.
36. The correct answer is D. The subject, "small houses", is plural, and the verb must be plural as well.
37. The correct answer is B, in which the initial independent clause is set off by a comma.
38. The correct answer is E, which avoids repeating the phrase "the neighborhood" twice within the same sentence.
39. The correct answer is D. "Individualness", in Choice A, is not a word. "Uniqueness" is the correct form which conveys the intended meaning: "individuality". Choices B, C, and E have the same meaning as "unity" and would make the sentence redundant.
40. The correct answer is A. Choice C would require use of the preposition "of", making "think of themselves as different".

Passage 3 – Poe

41. The correct answer is E, which is the past tense of the passive verb "to be born." Choice D is the passive past tense of the verb "to bear", meaning "to carry."
42. The correct answer is C. The plural form of the verb shows agreement with the subject. In choices B and D, "parent's" is possessive rather than plural.
43. The correct answer is A, which is a more formal usage than choice E, and more appropriate for a literary piece such as this excerpt.
44. The correct answer is B. Elizabeth was not pursuing the stress of supporting children, as expressed by choice A. Choice C is slang usage.
45. The correct answer is C. The disease name is not capitalized.
46. The correct answer is C. Here the adjective "only" has the meaning "merely", and emphasis is added by placing it immediately before the age, which it modifies.
47. The correct answer is B. The passage is written in the simple past tense, and in this choice the verb matches.
48. The correct answer is C, which is the correct form of the past tense.
49. The correct answer is D. The colon is used to introduce a capitalized quotation after a complete statement.

50. The correct answer is A. The word "want" can be used as a noun in addition to its usage as a verb.
51. The correct answer is D.
52. The correct answer is E. Here, the expression "not only…but also" is used with the correct form of the verb.
53. The correct answer is D, in which the modifying adverb is placed after the verbal expression "to take in".
54. The correct answer is C. Choice B, in which the verb is omitted, is slang usage.
55. The correct answer is C. Here, the expression "only added" means "added still more".
56. The correct answer is D. A prominent friend is a significant, important one.
57. The correct answer is E. Here, the first part of the sentence is a clause modifying the subject pronoun "she." In the original, the first sentence lacks a verb. The verb is also required to make the clause preceding a colon or semi-colon independent.
58. The correct answer is D. The form "whom" of the pronoun is used as the object of the verb.
59. The correct answer is B. Hyphens are used since the entire adjectival expression "14-year-old" is used to modify the noun.
60. The correct answer is B. The original form is a run-on sentence.

Secret Key #1 - Guessing is not Guesswork

You probably know that guessing is a good idea - unlike other standardized tests, there is no penalty for getting a wrong answer. Even if you have no idea about a question, you still have a 20-25% chance of getting it right.

Most test takers do not understand the impact that proper guessing can have on their score. Unless you score extremely high, guessing will significantly contribute to your final score.

Monkeys Take the Test

What most test takers don't realize is that to insure that 20-25% chance, you have to guess randomly. If you put 20 monkeys in a room to take this test, assuming they answered once per question and behaved themselves, on average they would get 20-25% of the questions correct. Put 20 test takers in the room, and the average will be much lower among guessed questions. Why?
1. The test writers intentionally writes deceptive answer choices that "look" right. A test taker has no idea about a question, so picks the "best looking" answer, which is often wrong. The monkey has no idea what looks good and what doesn't, so will consistently be lucky about 20-25% of the time.
2. Test takers will eliminate answer choices from the guessing pool based on a hunch or intuition. Simple but correct answers often get excluded, leaving a 0% chance of being correct. The monkey has no clue, and often gets lucky with the best choice.

This is why the process of elimination endorsed by most test courses is flawed and detrimental to your performance- test takers don't guess, they make an ignorant stab in the dark that is usually worse than random.

$5 Challenge

Let me introduce one of the most valuable ideas of this course- the $5 challenge:

You only mark your "best guess" if you are willing to bet $5 on it.
You only eliminate choices from guessing if you are willing to bet $5 on it.

Why $5? Five dollars is an amount of money that is small yet not insignificant, and can really add up fast (20 questions could cost you $100). Likewise, each answer choice on one question of the test will have a small impact on your overall score, but it can really add up to a lot of points in the end.

The process of elimination IS valuable. The following shows your chance of guessing it right:

If you eliminate wrong answer choices until only this many answer choices remain:	1	2	3

Chance of getting it correct:	100%	50%	33%

However, if you accidentally eliminate the right answer or go on a hunch for an incorrect answer, your chances drop dramatically: to 0%. By guessing among all the answer choices, you are GUARANTEED to have a shot at the right answer.

That's why the $5 test is so valuable- if you give up the advantage and safety of a pure guess, it had better be worth the risk.

What we still haven't covered is how to be sure that whatever guess you make is truly random. Here's the easiest way:

Always pick the first answer choice among those remaining.

Such a technique means that you have decided, **before you see a single test question**, exactly how you are going to guess- and since the order of choices tells you nothing about which one is correct, this guessing technique is perfectly random.

This section is not meant to scare you away from making educated guesses or eliminating choices- you just need to define when a choice is worth eliminating. The $5 test, along with a pre-defined random guessing strategy, is the best way to make sure you reap all of the benefits of guessing.

Secret Key #2 - Prepare, Don't Procrastinate

Let me state an obvious fact: if you take the test three times, you will get three different scores. This is due to the way you feel on test day, the level of preparedness you have, and, despite the test writers' claims to the contrary, some tests WILL be easier for you than others.

Since your future depends so much on your score, you should maximize your chances of success. In order to maximize the likelihood of success, you've got to prepare in advance. This means taking practice tests and spending time learning the information and test taking strategies you will need to succeed.

Never take the test as a "practice" test, expecting that you can just take it again if you need to. Feel free to take sample tests on your own, but when you go to take the official test, be prepared, be focused, and do your best the first time!

Secret Key #3 - Test Yourself

Everyone knows that time is money. There is no need to spend too much of your time or too little of your time preparing for the test. You should only spend as much of your precious time preparing as is necessary for you to get the score you need.

Once you have taken a practice test under real conditions of time constraints, then you will know if you are ready for the test or not.

If you have scored extremely high the first time that you take the practice test, then there is not much point in spending countless hours studying. You are already there.

Benchmark your abilities by retaking practice tests and seeing how much you have improved. Once you score high enough to guarantee success, then you are ready.

If you have scored well below where you need, then knuckle down and begin studying in earnest. Check your improvement regularly through the use of practice tests under real conditions. Above all, don't worry, panic, or give up. The key is perseverance!

Then, when you go to take the test, remain confident and remember how well you did on the practice tests. If you can score high enough on a practice test, then you can do the same on the real thing.

General Strategies

The most important thing you can do is to ignore your fears and jump into the test immediately- do not be overwhelmed by any strange-sounding terms. You have to jump into the test like jumping into a pool- all at once is the easiest way.

Make Predictions

As you read and understand the question, try to guess what the answer will be. Remember that several of the answer choices are wrong, and once you begin reading them, your mind will immediately become cluttered with answer choices designed to throw you off. Your mind is typically the most focused immediately after you have read the question and digested its contents. If you can, try to predict what the correct answer will be. You may be surprised at what you can predict.

Quickly scan the choices and see if your prediction is in the listed answer choices. If it is, then you can be quite confident that you have the right answer. It still won't hurt to check the other answer choices, but most of the time, you've got it!

Answer the Question

It may seem obvious to only pick answer choices that answer the question, but the test writers can create some excellent answer choices that are wrong. Don't pick an answer just because it sounds right, or you believe it to be true. It MUST answer the question. Once you've made your selection, always go back and check it against the question and make sure that you didn't misread the question, and the answer choice does answer the question posed.

Benchmark

After you read the first answer choice, decide if you think it sounds correct or not. If it doesn't, move on to the next answer choice. If it does, mentally mark that answer choice. This doesn't mean that you've definitely selected it as your answer choice, it just means that it's the best you've seen thus far. Go ahead and read the next choice. If the next choice is worse than the one you've already selected, keep going to the next answer choice. If the next choice is better than the choice you've already selected, mentally mark the new answer choice as your best guess.

The first answer choice that you select becomes your standard. Every other answer choice must be benchmarked against that standard. That choice is correct until proven otherwise by another answer choice beating it out. Once you've decided that no other answer choice seems as good, do one final check to ensure that your answer choice answers the question posed.

Valid Information

Don't discount any of the information provided in the question. Every piece of information may be necessary to determine the correct answer. None of the information in the question is there to throw you off (while the answer choices will certainly have information to throw you off). If two seemingly unrelated topics are discussed, don't ignore either. You can be confident there is a relationship, or it wouldn't be included in the question, and you are probably going to have to determine what is that relationship to find the answer.

Avoid "Fact Traps"

Don't get distracted by a choice that is factually true. Your search is for the answer that answers the question. Stay focused and don't fall for an answer that is true but incorrect. Always go back to the question and make sure you're choosing an answer that actually answers the question and is not just a true statement. An answer can be factually correct, but it MUST answer the question asked. Additionally, two answers can both be seemingly correct, so be sure to read all of the answer choices, and make sure that you get the one that BEST answers the question.

Milk the Question

Some of the questions may throw you completely off. They might deal with a subject you have not been exposed to, or one that you haven't reviewed in years. While your lack of knowledge about the subject will be a hindrance, the question itself can give you many clues that will help you find the correct answer. Read the question carefully and look for clues. Watch particularly for adjectives and nouns describing difficult terms or words that you don't recognize. Regardless of if you completely understand a word or not, replacing it with a synonym either provided or one you more familiar with may help you to understand what the questions are asking. Rather than wracking your mind about specific detailed information concerning a difficult term or word, try to use mental substitutes that are easier to understand.

The Trap of Familiarity

Don't just choose a word because you recognize it. On difficult questions, you may not recognize a number of words in the answer choices. The test writers don't put "make-believe" words on the test; so don't think that just because you only recognize all the words in one answer choice means that answer choice must be correct. If you only recognize words in one answer choice, then focus on that one. Is it correct? Try your best to determine if it is correct. If it is, that is great, but if it doesn't, eliminate it. Each word and answer choice you eliminate increases your chances of getting the question correct, even if you then have to guess among the unfamiliar choices.

Eliminate Answers

Eliminate choices as soon as you realize they are wrong. But be careful! Make sure you consider all of the possible answer choices. Just because one appears right, doesn't mean that the next one won't be even better! The test writers will usually put more than one good answer choice for every question, so read all of them. Don't worry if you are stuck between two that seem right. By getting down to just two remaining possible choices, your odds are now 50/50. Rather than wasting too much time, play the odds. You are guessing, but guessing wisely, because you've been able to knock out some of the answer choices that you know are wrong. If you are eliminating choices and realize that the last answer choice you are left with is also obviously wrong, don't panic. Start over and consider each choice again. There may easily be something that you missed the first time and will realize on the second pass.

Tough Questions

If you are stumped on a problem or it appears too hard or too difficult, don't waste time. Move on! Remember though, if you can quickly check for obviously incorrect answer choices, your chances of guessing correctly are greatly improved. Before you completely give up, at least try to knock out a couple of possible answers. Eliminate what you can and then guess at the remaining answer choices before moving on.

Brainstorm

If you get stuck on a difficult question, spend a few seconds quickly brainstorming. Run through the complete list of possible answer choices. Look at each choice and ask yourself, "Could this answer the question satisfactorily?" Go through each answer choice and consider it independently of the other. By systematically going through all possibilities, you may find something that you would otherwise overlook. Remember that when you get stuck, it's important to try to keep moving.

Read Carefully

Understand the problem. Read the question and answer choices carefully. Don't miss the question because you misread the terms. You have plenty of time to read each question thoroughly and make sure you understand what is being asked. Yet a happy medium must be attained, so don't waste too much time. You must read carefully, but efficiently.

Face Value

When in doubt, use common sense. Always accept the situation in the problem at face value. Don't read too much into it. These problems will not require you to make huge leaps of logic. The test writers aren't trying to throw you off with a cheap trick. If you have to go beyond creativity and make a leap of logic in order to have an answer choice answer the question, then you should look at the other answer choices. Don't overcomplicate the problem by creating theoretical relationships or explanations that will warp time or space. These are normal problems rooted in reality. It's just that the applicable relationship or explanation may not be readily apparent and you have to figure things out. Use your common sense to interpret anything that isn't clear.

Prefixes

If you're having trouble with a word in the question or answer choices, try dissecting it. Take advantage of every clue that the word might include. Prefixes and suffixes can be a huge help. Usually they allow you to determine a basic meaning. Pre- means before, post- means after, pro - is positive, de- is negative. From these prefixes and suffixes, you can get an idea of the general meaning of the word and try to put it into context. Beware though of any traps. Just because con is the opposite of pro, doesn't necessarily mean congress is the opposite of progress!

Hedge Phrases

Watch out for critical "hedge" phrases, such as likely, may, can, will often, sometimes, often, almost, mostly, usually, generally, rarely, sometimes. Question writers insert these hedge phrases to cover every possibility. Often an answer choice will be wrong simply because it leaves no room for exception. Avoid answer choices that have definitive words like "exactly," and "always".

Switchback Words

Stay alert for "switchbacks". These are the words and phrases frequently used to alert you to shifts in thought. The most common switchback word is "but". Others include although, however, nevertheless, on the other hand, even though, while, in spite of, despite, regardless of.

New Information

Correct answer choices will rarely have completely new information included. Answer choices typically are straightforward reflections of the material asked about and will directly relate to the question. If a new piece of information is included in an answer choice that doesn't even seem to relate to the topic being asked about, then that answer choice is likely incorrect. All of the information needed to answer the question is usually provided for you, and so you should not have to make guesses that are unsupported or choose answer choices that require unknown information that cannot be reasoned on its own.

Time Management

On technical questions, don't get lost on the technical terms. Don't spend too much time on any one question. If you don't know what a term means, then since you don't have a dictionary, odds are you aren't going to get much further. You should immediately recognize terms as whether or not you know them. If you don't, work with the other clues that you have, the other answer choices and terms provided, but don't waste too much time trying to figure out a difficult term.

Contextual Clues

Look for contextual clues. An answer can be right but not correct. The contextual clues will help you find the answer that is most right and is correct. Understand the context in which a phrase or statement is made. This will help you make important distinctions.

Don't Panic

Panicking will not answer any questions for you. Therefore, it isn't helpful. When you first see the question, if your mind goes blank, take a deep breath. Force yourself to mechanically go through the steps of solving the problem and using the strategies you've learned.

Answer Selection

The best way to pick an answer choice is to eliminate all of those that are wrong, until only one is left and confirm that is the correct answer. Sometimes though, an answer choice may immediately look right. Be careful! Take a second to make sure that the other choices are not equally obvious.

Don't make a hasty mistake.

Check Your Work

Since you will probably not know every term listed and the answer to every question, it is important that you get credit for the ones that you do know. Don't miss any questions through careless mistakes. If at all possible, try to take a second to look back over your answer selection and make sure you've selected the correct answer choice and haven't made a costly careless mistake (such as marking an answer choice that you didn't mean to mark). This quick double check should more than pay for itself in caught mistakes for the time it costs.

Beware of Directly Quoted Answers

Sometimes an answer choice will repeat word for word a portion of the question or reference section. However, beware of such exact duplication – it may be a trap! More than likely, the correct choice will paraphrase or summarize a point, rather than being exactly the same wording.

Slang

Scientific sounding answers are better than slang ones. An answer choice that begins "To compare the outcomes..." is much more likely to be correct than one that begins "Because some people insisted..."

Extreme Statements

Avoid wild answers that throw out highly controversial ideas that are proclaimed as established fact. An answer choice that states the "process should be used in certain situations, if..." is much more likely to be correct than one that states the "process should be discontinued completely." The first is a calm rational statement and doesn't even make a definitive, uncompromising stance, using a hedge word "if" to provide wiggle room, whereas the second choice is a radical idea and far more extreme.

Answer Choice Families

When you have two or more answer choices that are direct opposites or parallels, one of them is usually the correct answer. For instance, if one answer choice states "x increases" and another answer choice states "x decreases" or "y increases," then those two or three answer choices are very similar in construction and fall into the same family of answer choices. A family of answer choices is when two or three answer choices are very similar in construction, and yet often have a directly opposite meaning. Usually the correct answer choice will be in that family of answer choices. The "odd man out" or answer choice that doesn't seem to fit the parallel construction of the other answer choices is more likely to be incorrect.

Mathematics Appendix: Area, Volume, Surface Area Formulas

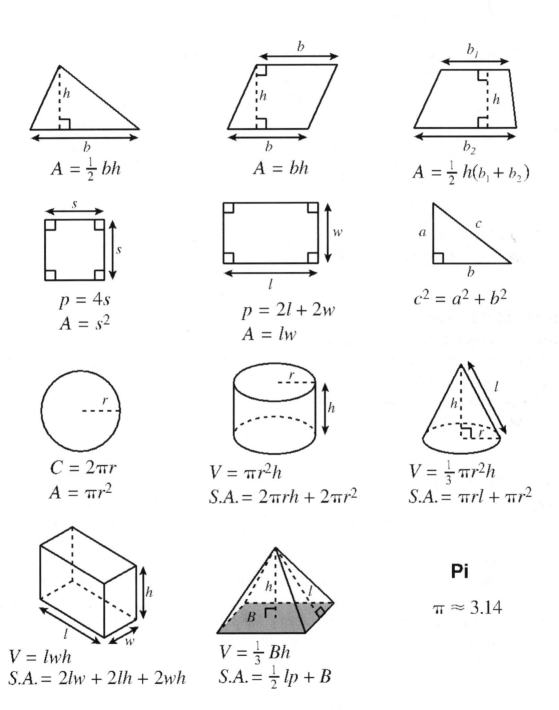

$A = \frac{1}{2}bh$

$A = bh$

$A = \frac{1}{2}h(b_1 + b_2)$

$p = 4s$
$A = s^2$

$p = 2l + 2w$
$A = lw$

$c^2 = a^2 + b^2$

$C = 2\pi r$
$A = \pi r^2$

$V = \pi r^2 h$
$S.A. = 2\pi rh + 2\pi r^2$

$V = \frac{1}{3}\pi r^2 h$
$S.A. = \pi rl + \pi r^2$

$V = lwh$
$S.A. = 2lw + 2lh + 2wh$

$V = \frac{1}{3}Bh$
$S.A. = \frac{1}{2}lp + B$

Pi

$\pi \approx 3.14$

Special Report: Additional Bonus Material

Due to our efforts to try to keep this book to a manageable length, we've created a link that will give you access to all of your additional bonus material.

Please visit http://www.mometrix.com/bonus948/compass to access the information.